Praise for
New Membership & Financ… for the American Synagogue

"The Rabbis Olitzky have faced head on what many of us are afraid to look at: for synagogues to survive they must change. Their compelling book is rooted in their love of synagogues, and it is their optimism about what is possible that allows them to examine models that, however radical, all suggest a vision of Jewish communal survival."

—**Rabbi Mychal Springer,** chair, professional and pastoral skills and director, Center for Pastoral Education, The Jewish Theological Seminary

"A very helpful, thorough guide for synagogue and Jewish communal leaders, clergy and prospective clergy.... A veritable playbook that addresses the key questions involved with each model, the pitfalls to be avoided and the process synagogue leadership must utilize to implement them.... A must-read for all who care about the future of synagogue affiliation and its financial stability ... in essence, the future of Jewish life in America."

—**Rabbi Norman Cohen,** professor emeritus of midrash, Hebrew Union College–Jewish Institute of Religion; author, *Believing and Its Tensions: A Personal Conversation about God, Torah, Suffering and Death in Jewish Thought*

"Offers new thinking and new models of affiliation. Whether we are committed to old ways or searching for new ones, this work will provoke reflection and open possibilities."

—**Dr. Steven M. Cohen,** research professor of Jewish social policy, Hebrew Union College–Jewish Institute of Religion

"Finally, a book that not only explains the challenges facing American synagogues today, but actually offers realistic, creative and constructive ways to overcome them.... Give[s] synagogues of every size the tools and the confidence to look beyond what is—to what needs to be."

—**Rabbi David Rosen,** senior rabbi, Congregation Beth Yeshurun, Houston, Texas

"[The] Rabbis Olitzky ... ask critical questions and suggest bold solutions, all in the service of vitalizing synagogues.... A helpful sourcebook for important conversations."

—**Rabbi Deborah Waxman, PhD**, president, Reconstructionist Rabbinical College and Jewish Reconstructionist Communities

"Packed with clarifying ideas and refreshing experiments, encourages us to get ahead of the curve, to be ambitious in our aspirations."

—**Rabbi Yael Splansky,** Holy Blossom Temple, Toronto, Ontario; author, URJ's "Reform Voices of Torah: 2012 Commentary on Deuteronomy"

"Instead of focusing on the doom and gloom of synagogue life, the Rabbis Olitzky write a practical and common 'cents' book about how our temple communities can grow and thrive."

—**Craig Taubman,** musician; founder, Pico Union Project, Los Angeles, California

"Honestly, lovingly and productively examines the difficult issue of synagogue membership.... An intelligent and well-balanced book, based on careful research.... Should be a requirement for all rabbis, lay leaders and rabbinical students to read, ponder and begin to think about what the future of their organization should look like."

—**Rabbi Asher Lopatin,** president, Yeshivat Chovevei Torah Rabbinical School

New Membership & Financial Alternatives for the American Synagogue

From Traditional Dues to Fair Share to Gifts from the Heart

Rabbi Kerry M. Olitzky & Rabbi Avi S. Olitzky

Foreword by Dr. Ron Wolfson

Afterword by Rabbi Dan Judson

For People of All Faiths, All Backgrounds

JEWISH LIGHTS Publishing

Woodstock, Vermont

www.jewishlights.com

New Membership & Financial Alternatives for the American Synagogue: From Traditional Dues to Fair Share to Gifts from the Heart

2015 Quality Paperback Edition, First Printing

Biblical and Talmudic translations are the authors', unless otherwise indicated.

Library of Congress Cataloging-in-Publication Data
Olitzky, Kerry M., author.
New membership & financial alternatives for the American synagogue : from traditional dues to fair share to gifts from the heart / Rabbi Kerry M. Olitzky ; Rabbi Avi S. Olitzky ; foreword by Dr. Ron Wolfson ; afterword by Rabbi Dan Judson.
pages cm
Includes bibliographical references.
ISBN 978-1-58023-820-5 (quality pb) —ISBN 978-1-58023-828-1 (ebook) 1. Synagogues—United States—Finance. 2. Synagogues—United States—Membership 3. Synagogues—United States—Organization and administration. I. Olitzky, Avi S., 1981– author. II. Title. III. Title: New membership and financial alternatives for the American synagogue.
BM653.3.O45 2015
296.6'5—dc23

2014047469

10 9 8 7 6 5 4 3 2 1

Manufactured in the United States of America
Cover and interior design: Michael Myers
Cover art: Shutterstock Image 141436108, modified by Michael Myers

For People of All Faiths, All Backgrounds
Jewish Lights Publishing
A Division of LongHill Partners, Inc.
Sunset Farm Offices, Route 4, P.O. Box 237
Woodstock, VT 05091
Tel: (802) 457-4000 Fax: (802) 457-4004
www.jewishlights.com

For Sheryl Olitzky and for Sarah Olitzky,
our life partners and best friends

Build for Me a sanctuary, but I will dwell in your midst.

Exodus 25:8

You should not appear before God empty-handed. Every person should give in accordance with how he [or she] has been blessed by God.

Deuteronomy 16:16b–17

Congregations are a lot like homes; you get what you pay for ... there are no substitutes for investing in and maintaining something of quality and lasting value.

Rabbi Lawrence Kushner[1]

Rabbi Ishmael said: One who wishes to acquire wisdom should study the way that money works, for there is no greater area of Torah study than this.

Babylonian Talmud, *Bava Batra* 175b

Contents

Who Should Read This Book

- Synagogue board members
- Synagogue professional staff, including rabbis, cantors, educators, and executive directors
- Jewish communal leaders, especially Jewish Federation planning directors
- Jewish communal service and rabbinical students
- Anyone interested in the future of the North American Jewish community and the synagogue

How to Use This Book

- Use this book as a stimulus and guide for your own synagogue's discussion of change in membership models and dues structures.
- Devote time at synagogue board meetings for a discussion of each model in this volume.
- Use the table of contents as a broad outline for a synagogue board retreat.
- Provide the opportunity for discussion of each model by describing them in an interactive section on your synagogue's website.
- Include the book as required reading in a class on Jewish communal planning and the future of the synagogue.

Foreword

Of the many challenges facing synagogues, securing the financial resources to sustain them is often at the top of the list for congregational leaders. After all, if the congregation fails to raise the dollars to pay for the organizational infrastructure, facilities, schools, programs, clergy, educators, and staff, the synagogue could very well face merger or even closure. For more than a century, the North American synagogue has depended on annual dues from members to fund these costs. Increasingly, synagogue leaders report resistance to this model of collecting revenue. Are there other options for raising the money? Indeed, are there even new ways to think about the very idea of "membership" in synagogues?

These two compelling questions are at the heart of this welcome addition to the growing conversation about synagogue membership models and financial alternatives. Rabbis Kerry M. Olitzky and Avi S. Olitzky have done their homework. Not only do they cite interesting revenue-generating models from the general culture, but the book is also replete with examples of synagogues, independent minyanim, and spiritual communities that have developed creative and sometimes surprising strategies for rethinking both the concept of membership and how congregations can build revenue streams that ameliorate what many observers believe are obstacles to recruiting and engaging Jews into their spiritual communities.

The most cited obstacle to synagogue membership is the cost. "Why do we have to pay to pray?" asks the potential member. I once heard Rabbi Edward Feinstein of Valley Beth Shalom in Encino, California, answer the question bluntly:

> You don't have to pay to pray. But, if you want heat in the building on Hanukkah and air-conditioning on Yom Kippur, there is a cost. If you want a prayer book, there is a cost. If you want a rabbi and a cantor to be there for you, there is a cost. If you want teachers for your children, there is a cost. For 362 days of the year, our doors are wide open for anyone who wants to pray—without cost. For a synagogue to provide these services, there is a cost ... and it is our members who generously offer gifts from their heart—we call them "dues"—to support this effort.[2]

This is a cogent argument, but there is a necessary next step. Synagogues are notoriously reticent to reveal their budgets to anyone other than the boards of directors and senior staff. There may be a general discussion of the budget at the congregational annual meeting, but often it is not well attended. Very few congregations post their balance sheets on the synagogue website. There is no need to publicize individual salaries, but synagogues would be well served to be more transparent about the real costs of running the organization. Unlike 501(c)(3) charities, synagogues are classified by the Internal Revenue Service as religious institutions, excused from reporting their financial condition.

There are, of course, deeper issues in play. Our authors are unafraid to ask the fundamental question: Why membership? They point to Chabad—the best-known, most successful Jewish outreach and engagement organization in the Jewish world—which turned the membership-and-dues model upside down. Instead of "Pay dues and be served," their strategy is "We will serve you, and then we'll ask you for money"—which Chabad rabbis aggressively and often effectively do.

The Olitzkys then turn to another important question: What is the relationship between member and organization? Is it simply transactional? The member thinks, "The synagogue offers me a 'product' and a 'service' that I pay for ... and when I no longer need or want your product or service, I quit." Unfortunately, a transactional relationship is the defining characteristic of most of our culture, including synagogues. If I don't perceive "value" in what I receive for my support, I am unlikely to continue paying. Similarly, if I don't "use" the synagogue anymore—I don't go to services, my kids are post–bar mitzvah—why keep up my membership?

"Value" is the underlying question at hand. Once, the value of supporting a synagogue was a widely accepted norm among the majority of North American Jews, who established the several thousand synagogues that at one time attracted some 80 percent of them as members for at least some part of their lives. In many communities, even those who didn't "use" the synagogue except for a few days a year of prayer and occasional life-cycle events nevertheless accepted the idea that supporting a congregation is a communal responsibility. As the Rabbis Olitzky correctly point out, the Torah itself recognizes the importance of sustaining the religious institutions of the community. In Exodus, each person, rich or poor, is instructed to give "half a shekel," along with mandatory "sin offerings" and voluntary "gifts from the heart," depending on one's talents and abilities. The bottom line is that the bottom line was funded by a universal tax.

Regrettably, those days are over. And so synagogues scramble to provide "value-able" products and services to entice membership: schools for children, bar/bat mitzvah preparation and celebration, and all kinds of programs, along with prayer experiences. But if I can get my kid bar/bat mitzvah tutoring online for much less than school tuitions, if I can hire an independent rabbi to officiate at life-cycle events, if I can go to "pop-up" High Holy Day services offered for a few hundred dollars, and if I can watch live streaming of weekly and holiday worship in my pajamas, why join a synagogue?

As I argue in *Relational Judaism: Using the Power of Relationships to Transform the Jewish Community* (Jewish Lights), the value proposition of synagogues must change. If the value offered is a calendar of programs, access to Jewish information, cultural events, even activities to "repair the world," our people can get all that for much less money than the cost of synagogue affiliation. But if our value proposition is the opportunity to be in face-to-face meaningful relationship with Jews and Judaism in a relational, not transactional, community that offers a path to meaning and purpose, belonging and blessing, we have a shot at engaging our people in a twenty-first-century relational Judaism.

If this then is our goal, the opportunity afforded us in this challenging book to think out of the box about membership models and revenue strategies is of the moment. As I visit synagogues across North America, meeting with boards of directors, these are the crucial questions being asked and debated.

Be warned: this book has the potential to shake long-held beliefs about how synagogue membership is counted and courted. The authors duly recognize this by offering advice on how to avoid the stumbling blocks of adopting or adapting any one of the new models they present. They understand that to change cultural expectations and norms is enormously difficult. They do not favor one model over another; rather, they present examples of pioneering synagogues that have been willing to take the risk of forging a new approach. Will they work for your synagogue? It will depend on a number of factors. I do know that most synagogue leaders will be duly cautious and that success will only come when there is a careful, thoughtful, and thorough process, centered on community conversations about the meaning of membership and the culture of money. Reading and discussing this resourceful book is an excellent way to facilitate that important work.

Dr. Ron Wolfson
Fingerhut Professor of Education,
American Jewish University
Cofounder, Synagogue 3000
Author, *Relational Judaism: Using the Power of Relationships to Transform the Jewish Community* (Jewish Lights)

Acknowledgments

There are so many people to thank for their assistance in bringing together the ideas in this book. If we have neglected to acknowledge anyone by name, we apologize in advance. We have tried to include many examples of synagogues that have changed their membership and revenue models. However, to those who are boldly moving forward and were not included in this book, please forgive us the oversight. We applaud you for taking the important risks nonetheless.

In particular, we thank the following people for their help in confirming various details included in this book, as well as for making suggestions: Dr. David Ackerman and Allan Finkelstein, Jewish Community Center Association; Melanie Adler and Allison Hausman of Congregation Dorshei Tzedek in West Newton, Massachusetts; Jessica Antoline and Rabbi Sam Seicol at the Vilna Shul in Boston, Massachusetts; Rabbi Shoshanah Conover and Rabbi Edwin Goldberg of Temple Sholom in Chicago, Illinois; Rabbi Neil Cooper of Temple Beth Hillel–Beth El in Wynnewood, Pennsylvania; Rabbi Bruce Diamond of the Community Free Synagogue of Fort Myers, Florida; Esther Safran Foer, executive director, Sixth & I Synagogue in Washington, DC; Cantor Adina H. Frydman of Synergy: UJA–Federation in New York and Synagogues Together; Rabbi Linda Henry Goodman of Union Temple in Brooklyn, New York; Rabbi Samuel Gordon of Sukkat Shalom in Wilmette, Illinois; Dr. Judith Hauptman, E. Billi Ivry Professor of Talmud and Rabbinic Culture at The Jewish Theological Seminary and rabbi of Ohel Ayalah in the New York City area; Rabbi Lizzi Heydemann of Mishkan Chicago; Rabbi Elie Kaunfer of Mechon Hadar in New York, New York; Anna Kohn of the Isaac Agree Downtown Synagogue in Detroit, Michigan;

Naomi Less of the Lab/Shul in New York, New York; Rabbi Darren Levine of Tamid: The Downtown Synagogue, New York, New York; Rabbi Naomi Levy of Nashuva in Los Angeles, California; Rabbi Adina Lewittes of Sha'ar Communities in New Jersey; Lee Livingston, former president of Anshe Emeth Memorial Temple in New Brunswick, New Jersey; Rabbi David Lyon of Congregation Beth Israel in Houston, Texas; Rabbi Steven S. Mason of North Shore Congregation Israel in Glencoe, Illinois; Rabbi David J. Meyer of Temple Emanu-El in Marblehead, Massachusetts; Rabbi Jack Moline of the National Jewish Democratic Council; Rabbi Michael Namath and Isaac Nuell of the Religious Action Center of Reform Judaism; Rabbi Robert Nosanchuk of Congregation Anshe Chesed/Fairmount Temple in Cleveland, Ohio; Rabbi Marc Philippe of Temple Emanu-El in Miami Beach, Florida; Rabbi Leonard Rosenthal of Tifereth Israel Synagogue in San Carlos, California; Rabbi Don Rosoff of Temple B'nai Or in Morristown, New Jersey; Patti Wasserburger Nisenholz and Becky Adelberg of the JCC Chicago; and Rabbi Michael Wasserman of The New Shul in Scottsdale, Arizona.

The pioneering scholarship of Rabbi Dan Judson must be acknowledged. His work is reflected in the changes made by some of the institutions that are included in this book. We also thank him for his insightful afterword.

In addition, we thank Debbie Joseph for her helpful practical lists that we have included in this book.

We also extend deep appreciation to Dr. Ron Wolfson for writing the foreword. His *Relational Judaism: Using the Power of Relationships to Transform the Jewish Community* (Jewish Lights) has already made a significant impact on many synagogues. In some ways, this book is an extension of his important contribution to Jewish life and the synagogue.

Additional thanks go to Rabbi Alexander Davis, John Orenstein, and Linda Goldberg of Beth El Synagogue in St. Louis Park, Minnesota, who responded to various ideas mentioned in this book.

We have to single out Stuart M. Matlins, publisher and editor in chief of Jewish Lights, friend, and cofounder with his wife, Antoinette, of the oldest, most successful no dues/no fees synagogue

synagogue in the country in Woodstock, Vermont, who helped us shape this book and its content. We also thank Emily Wichland, Rachel Shields, and the entire staff at Jewish Lights Publishing for all they do to help bring our words and message to life on the page and beyond. A special thanks to our editor Beth Gaede for helping us find the best way to express what we wanted to say.

We also express our gratitude to the many participants in training sessions and workshops sponsored by Big Tent Judaism/Jewish Outreach Institute, where many of these ideas were first presented; to the congregants of Beth El Synagogue in St. Louis Park, Minnesota; and to those at Shaaray Torah Synagogue in Canton, Ohio. Moreover, we thank the staff of Big Tent Judaism/Jewish Outreach Institute, members of its board, and president, Michael Rappeport, who refuse to allow for "business as usual" as we work to build a more inclusive Jewish community. In particular, we thank Paul Golin, associate executive director, for reviewing some of the material and making helpful suggestions along the way.

We also celebrate the efforts of synagogue leaders who are helping to bring forward the next iteration of synagogue life. Most important, this book has allowed our many conversations—of father and son—to find concrete expression in these pages.

We also thank our family for their support of our efforts—and their support of us—especially when we face criticism in response to provocative ideas that form the foundation of our work.

Above all, we give thanks to the Omnipresent, for whom we all labor.

Don't destroy the old synagogue before you build anew.

Babylonian Talmud, *Bava Batra* 3b

Jews need one another, and therefore congregations, to do primary religious acts that they should not, and probably cannot, do alone. Doing primary religious acts is the only way we have of growing as Jews. Consequently, it is also the only justification for the existence of a congregation. Everything else congregations do, Jews can always do cheaper, easier, and better somewhere else.

Rabbi Lawrence Kushner[1]

Introduction

This book is about synagogues, institutions we both love and support, which have carried the Jewish people far into their religious journey and nurtured us well into our own. It is designed to help those who, like us, believe in synagogues and want them to continue to survive and succeed. The synagogue affiliation and revenue models we present offer possibilities that individual congregations can adopt and adapt to meet their needs.

Our goal is to provide synagogue and communal leaders with a thoughtful process and the ingredients necessary to consider important changes in the synagogue. Some synagogue leaders will be motivated to change membership models because of the financial implications, but our motivation is far more basic. It is not just financial. Our goal is to show synagogue leaders how to welcome into membership those who are currently not engaged in synagogue life and the Jewish community.

Because we believe in the religious community of the synagogue, we want to find ways to bring people to the synagogue and keep them there. We also want to change the way synagogue leaders and members think about dues, to drop the image of dues as a form of taxation—which few people actually enjoy paying—and to promote the notion that dues are an expression of philanthropy, giving from the heart, which has the potential to elevate the soul. Because of financial and demographic challenges, some institutions are being forced against their will to make structural changes. This book provides synagogue and communal leaders with the ingredients necessary to make changes and even to see the necessary changes as an opportunity for growth and exciting innovations.

The contemporary membership model for synagogues, whose financial foundation depends primarily on members paying dues and contributing to additional fundraising efforts, is an innovation dating back to the latter part of the nineteenth century, when churches were asking for weekly offerings and using a collection plate. Charging dues allowed synagogues to more accurately project their annual revenue and plan for the congregations they had formed. Like members of Protestant churches, Jewish community members voluntarily came together to form synagogues. Establishing congregations was especially important when the non-Jewish world was not friendly or welcoming to them. Membership in a synagogue brought Jewish people closer to one another. While many people think most Jews are synagogue members—and that may have once been the case in some locations—the majority of Jews in a neighborhood or community seldom join synagogues. Nevertheless, there are more synagogues than any other Jewish communal institution in the United States and Canada.

While the membership-and-dues model still sustains some synagogues, its decline in the past twenty-five years is threatening the financial viability of many synagogues. The majority of synagogues in the United States are looking to a diminishing membership base to meet their expenses. According to a 2013 Pew Research Center Study, only 31 percent of American Jews belong to synagogues.[2] The National Jewish Population Study reported synagogue membership at 46 percent in 2001.[3] That is a decrease of 15 percent in just over a decade. While the two studies are not directly comparable in terms of their methodology, this decrease is nevertheless suggestive.[4] Dues increases have helped mitigate the financial loss because of a decrease in the number of members, but asking fewer members to pay more is not a sustainable approach. Thus, the dues-paying membership model can no longer broadly support the North American synagogue. The system must be reconsidered.

Some synagogue leaders blame the decline of synagogue membership on the deterioration of the American economy, particularly since the recession of 2008. Others suggest that the loss of membership is a result of demographic shifts in North America. For example, people are growing older, having fewer children, and moving out of the neighborhoods where synagogues are located. While these factors have had a substantial impact on the organized Jewish community and have contributed to the loss of members, synagogues are shrinking for many other reasons. Some of the factors that have forced synagogue leaders to reflect on the mission and purpose of the contemporary synagogue will be discussed in this book. However, rather than providing an extensive analysis of the problem and its origins, we will focus on ways to address these challenges so readers can consider a broad range of alternatives to the familiar synagogue membership-and-dues structure. Which changes to explore and how to make those changes are the major themes of this book.

Change does not come easily to any institution, large or small, however. The most active and involved congregants interpret the need for change as a challenge to the status quo and, ironically, given their high level of support for the synagogue's mission, become the greatest obstacles to change. Thus, volunteer and rabbinic leadership with a strong vision will need to mobilize a team of synagogue members to translate the mission into action and enlist members of the congregation as partners to successfully implement a new model. Without the support of the congregation, irrespective of the merit of the vision, the change implementation may not succeed.

Determining who may participate as a member in synagogue activities and ritual life, as well as in legal decision making, is critical to the realization of the synagogue's vision. It is also the fundamental issue that all of the synagogue affiliation and revenue models in this book address in different ways. Of course, if a synagogue dispenses with any form of membership, an idea that will be discussed in chapter 6, the issue of who is a member may be irrelevant. Nevertheless, as synagogues consider the various affiliation and revenue models they could adopt, they also have to think about which segments of the population will be attracted to and can be easily included in the chosen model. This is particularly important given the increase in our communities in the number of interfaith families, as well as the changing family structures that are replacing the normative family that has been the focus of the synagogue community and its programs.

Besides their role as religious communities, synagogues are also legal entities. Members may have to vote to adopt any new membership structure for their synagogue. In any case, the definition of membership and the member's legal role in the life of the congregation must always be taken into consideration when adopting a new affiliation and revenue model. The reason is simple: who can vote and on what will determine future congregational activity and leadership, including who is retained as rabbi. Ultimately, the definition of membership goes beyond legal issues. It has implications for everything the synagogue does.

In this book, we first present a brief history of the synagogue and its role and value in the Jewish community. We then offer an overview of the dues-paying membership model and explore why it is under siege and failing in some places. Next we provide a series of alternatives to guide synagogue leaders who realize they have to change the dominant dues-based membership model but have no idea how to change it or how they would mitigate the risks of various alternatives. Some of the models we describe have been successfully implemented in North American synagogues. In our descriptions, we classify synagogues by the size of their membership: up to 400, small; up to 750, medium; over 1,000, large. To stimulate creative thinking, examples from the commercial world are also included. The information in this book comes from a variety of sources, including, but not limited to, interviews with synagogue leaders and synagogue websites. For more in-depth information, you may contact the individual synagogues, as well as consulting the resources contained at the conclusion of this book.

At the conclusion of each chapter, we have included highlights, frequently asked questions, and implementation steps for each model. In the appendices, we include checklists to help determine which model to choose for your synagogue, as well as lists of things to do following the decision to adopt a new model and twenty-five reasons to join synagogues. This list is meant to stimulate discussion among synagogue leaders, who can customize and explicate the list as it pertains to individual synagogues and ponder what may attract new participants and members to engage in these synagogues.

If you are experimenting with models that are not described in this book, please let us know. We want to learn more about them and consider including them in the next edition so that others might share in your creativity and success.

The *Shekhina* is in the synagogue even when one person is there.

Mekhilta to Exodus 20:21

Why synagogue? To carve out a spacious safe space deep within our busy lives, making room for mystery to dwell, for compassion to blossom, human vulnerability to echo and a deeper connection celebrated with all of our body, all of our being, and all of our soul.

Amichai Lau-Lavie[1]

1

The Shifting Relationship of the Synagogue and the Jewish Community

The synagogue is the spiritual touchstone for the Jewish community. It is the place where Jews and their families can join together to access the holy in their lives and grow closer to the Divine. Of course, people join synagogues for many other reasons. Following World War II, people moved to the suburbs and established families there. Because they wanted to continue their Jewish religious and ritual life, Jewishly educate their children, and in some cases, establish professional and social contacts and replace the community they left behind, they formed synagogues.

During the early post–World War II period, many of these suburban Jews considered synagogue membership an obligation. People felt obligated to support Jewish communal institutions and considered such support an affirmation of the rightful place of Jews in the community. That sense of obligation has waned because the Jews' place as being fully American is no longer being challenged, especially among the millennial generation.

As a result, synagogue members increasingly want to know the costs and benefits of their membership. Rather than asking, "How shall I meet my obligation to financially support the synagogue?" a member may ask, "Is the amount of money I am spending for my membership worth it? What am *I* getting out of the money I am spending for synagogue membership?"

The cost for synagogue membership has increased while its benefit has diminished over time for many, seeming to make synagogue membership "not worth it." Members no longer seem to want what some synagogues have to offer. Moreover, they can get elsewhere many of the services that are offered by synagogues. Certainly few people today speak about synagogue membership as a reflection of their rightful place in the community.

Today an increasing number of people don't want to feel obligated to give to the synagogue. They generally want the opportunity to give freely, from the heart, and not out of a sense of duty. And they want to see tangible results from their gift. Consequently, we believe that synagogue leaders have to be prepared to answer the question "Why should we support the synagogue?" According to Ron Wolfson, based on his groundbreaking *Relational Judaism*, a person should be able to ask:

Does my synagogue

1. Change my life?
2. Strengthen my family?
3. Give me a community of friends to celebrate the ups and downs of my life?
4. Teach me how to use Jewish study and practice to enhance my life?
5. Connect me to both a sacred and a civic Jewish community in a significant way?
6. Give me a sense of belonging to the Jewish people?
7. Deepen my relationship with the State of Israel?
8. Lead me to do the work of repairing the world?
9. Help me to build a relationship with God, however I define God?[2]

Just as synagogues play an important role in the life of the individual, they also are important to the Jewish community. Synagogues were once built in the physical heart of a Jewish community. Jews who lived in the neighborhood participated in them as the religious center of Jewish life. These synagogues served as cultural centers and gathering places as well, because the wider community did not welcome Jews. As these synagogues grew, the Jewish community grew around them.

The neighborhood synagogue has disappeared in the majority of Jewish communities today, however, and the so-called Jewish community may be spread over a large geographic area even in one city. Of course, members of Jewish religious movements and synagogues whose adherents will only walk to their synagogue on Shabbat and holidays are not geographically dispersed. Their members necessarily make their homes close to the synagogue. It is also true that some other synagogues have pockets of member households who still live nearby, even if these members will use automobiles on Shabbat.

Rabbi Eric Yoffie, the former president of the Union for Reform Judaism, has offered his own reasons for the perpetuation of synagogues, adding to Wolfson's list. Why synagogue? He responds:

> The synagogue is the only place in the Jewish world that can be counted on to care about the individual Jew, and where everyone, no matter how rich or poor, is valued as having been created in the image of God. It is the place that attends to the pain of its members, celebrates their successes, and provides the loving embrace of community. It is the only Jewish institution that is truly democratic and takes pride in its grassroots character. And it is a place of prayer and study for Jews of every age. No other Jewish institution does these things, and none will.[3]

Amichai Lau-Lavie, the founder of Storahtelling (an educational drama troupe that interprets the weekly Torah reading) and the Lab/Shul in Manhattan, and currently a rabbinical student at The Jewish Theological Seminary, offers some suggestions for the perpetuation of the synagogue. (See chapter 8 for more information on the Lab/Shul.) Why synagogue? Lau-Lavie tells us that the synagogue helps "to carve out a spacious safe space deep within our busy lives, making room for mystery to dwell, for compassion to blossom, human vulnerability to echo and a deeper connection celebrated with all of our body, all of our being, and all of our soul."

Finally, Rabbi David Cohen of Congregation Sinai (Reform) in Milwaukee, Wisconsin, suggests that synagogues exist to meet three basic human needs: the need to belong, the need to believe, and the need to become.

All of these leaders view the synagogue as a place to help the individual embrace the sacred, mark life's individual transitions, and support the quest to find his or her place in the community. In addition, we should keep in mind the historical definition of the three purposes of a synagogue as a house of prayer, study, and assembly.

Communal Support for the Synagogue

A personal desire to support the synagogue does not emerge merely from a sense of responsibility felt by the individual. Rather, the obligation to support the community is derived from the Torah, where the ancient Israelites are directed to support the desert Tabernacle and later the Temple in Jerusalem: "The rich shall not pay more and the poor shall not pay less than half a shekel when giving the Eternal One's offering" (Exodus 30:15). This half shekel was considered to be an affordable amount, allowing all people access to the central place of worship, irrespective of tribe or economic class.

But the half shekel was inadequate to support all the activities of the Temple cult, so the ancient community began asking for voluntary offerings, along with various mandatory offerings, including the sin offering, as prescribed in the Torah. According to Rabbi Lester Bronstein of Bet Am Shalom (Reconstructionist) in White Plains, New York, individuals gave to support the ancient Tabernacle because they had a personal sense that they mattered to the community. The community valued their presence and ongoing contributions to the community. Rabbi Bronstein suggests that the term *terumah* (literally, an elevation offering) was used to refer to the offering because it emphasized the giver's worth to the community. This prompted the individual, says Rabbi Bronstein, to stay involved in the community and to keep giving over the entirety of the person's life.

The Exodus model of taxing individuals to support the community followed the Jewish people throughout its history. The membership model of the contemporary synagogue emerged in part from the notion that all people who belong to a community are obligated to support it. In some Jewish communities today, such as in Germany, variations on the Exodus model are still in place. German Jews can elect to add a percentage to their income tax to be distributed to a federal entity that supports communal institutions, synagogues, and rabbis. In Hungary, a portion of everyone's income tax is involuntarily collected for the support of religious institutions recognized by the government.

Funds collected by the community to support its institutions were probably never adequate, nor has collecting community taxes or dues been a universal practice, so throughout history other methods have been used. For example, beginning in the fourteenth century in Europe, Torah honors were sold to provide funds for the synagogue, a practice later eschewed by the Reform movement in principle as being elitist and privileging the wealthy in the synagogue, thus undermining a basic Reform principle of egalitarianism.

Congregation B'nai Jeshurun, today a vibrant institution on Manhattan's Upper West Side, was established as a result of a conflict over selling Torah honors. It seems that in 1825 Barrow Cohen, a member of the synagogue, was called to the Torah in New York's Congregation Shearith Israel, the only synagogue in New York at the time. Cohen refused to pledge a donation in exchange for the honor—declining to follow the prevailing practice at the synagogue. The synagogue's board of directors brought him to "trial" and censured him for his actions. Cohen raised the issue among other members, and together they pushed back against the synagogue's board. While the board was willing to reduce the cost of the *aliyah* (the honor of saying a blessing at the Torah), it was insufficient to address the economic inequality as seen by the synagogue's critics. As a result, this group of members left Shearith Israel to form B'nai Jeshurun.

The practice of selling honors has generally fallen out of favor in the Jewish community, except in some Orthodox synagogues and often only on special occasions and holidays, but funds have been collected in other ways. For a time, synagogue leaders, such as those at Shearith Israel mentioned above, attempted to collect funds from congregants based on personal wealth. They also tried selling seats in the synagogue. When that proved unsuccessful after a period of time, they then rented synagogue seats to members. Nothing seemed effective, though, and any method that worked initially was not effective for an extended period of time. So they kept changing their methods, with varying success.

By the early part of the twentieth century, the Reform movement chose, once again on principle, to discontinue the practice of what they called "selling seats," or requiring members to pay for reserved seats. This led to the implementation of obligatory dues. For these early reformers, the practice of selling seats flew in the face of American democracy and the egalitarian nature of the Reform movement. Nevertheless, it returned later in Reform synagogues under the guise of selling tickets for the High Holy Days—even when it was a privilege open only to dues-paying members.

Soon the High Holy Day appeal, still a practice in many synagogues, was adopted as a significant fundraising apparatus to complement the collection of dues, irrespective of religious movement affiliation. In some synagogues, these High Holy Day appeals fund the social justice work of the synagogue rather than its operating budget. Such is the case, for example, at Congregation Beth Israel (Reform) in West Hartford, Connecticut, and Congregation Emanu-El (Reform) in New York City. At the same time, in the early part of the twentieth century, mushroom synagogues, as they were called because they sprouted up overnight, developed. They were established as what we might now call "pop-ups" (akin to contemporary models discussed in chapter 6). However, the mushroom synagogues were for-profit enterprises that took advantage of those Jews who wanted only to attend High Holy Day services. These services were often held in Yiddish theaters and saloons. Organizers sold their seats at a price lower than other neighborhood synagogues. In response, the established Jewish communal institutions successfully lobbied the New York State Legislature in the 1930s to outlaw these institutions in New York (where almost all of them existed, because of the concentration of the Jewish population).

While synagogues use High Holy Day services for revenue, even those synagogues that charge for High Holy Day tickets operate under the assumption that everyone is welcome to attend weekly worship services, regardless of their ability to pay dues. Nevertheless, to obtain a reduction in dues, synagogues often require members to fill out extensive forms that request financial information and are subject to a committee review. Some synagogues go as far as to request income tax returns. Most synagogues have what they call a "dues forgiveness policy," which allows even those who are unable to pay the full amount of dues to become members or maintain their membership. But there is an implicit social stigma attached in some institutions to those members who pay less than the full amount of dues. As a result, many do not request dues reduction and instead either never join the synagogue or resign when they are unable to pay for their membership. The avoidance behavior of such individuals who are potential members further emphasizes the need to secure alternative methods for revenue sources to support the synagogue.

Why Consider a New Model for Synagogue Affiliation and Revenue?

Simply put, a new model for synagogue affiliation and revenue should be considered because the old model is no longer working well. Fewer people are joining synagogues, and more demands to support the synagogue are being made on those who do belong. Some critics of the new models explored in this book will suggest that the old model could work if only we instilled a sense of duty in those who no longer feel obligated to support synagogues. Once we do so, goes the argument, synagogues will have no problem maintaining the membership-and-dues status quo. These same critics who argue that the solution to synagogues' woes is a renewed sense of obligation suggest that synagogues face only economic problems. In other words, if synagogues had the funds they needed to operate, all would be fine. Nothing else about the synagogue would need to change.

Other factors prompt the need to consider changing the synagogue membership and revenue model, however. For example,

Jews can fulfill their Jewish needs outside of the synagogue. No longer is Judaism restricted to mainstream Jewish communal institutions. Myriad resources are available in the community (many on the Internet) that do not require membership in a synagogue, any prior Jewish literacy, a Jewish identity that is affirmed by all Jewish religious movements (especially important for intermarried families with children of patrilineal descent), or any kind of long-term financial commitment. Rethinking the synagogue model can help synagogue leaders meet the needs of those currently not served by the synagogue, particularly those who have been historically disenfranchised by the synagogue community or who are simply not interested in the current panoply of programs and service offerings. By turning the synagogue "inside out" and programming in public spaces, for example, the synagogue can become an institution that serves the entire community rather than focusing solely on the needs of its current members. The needs of spiritual seekers ought to be addressed as well, along with the needs of those for whom Jewish thought and ideas—separate from Judaism as religion—spark an interest.

Moreover, innovations in the synagogue are needed because such changes help make Judaism more accessible and more relevant to the millennial generation, Gen X, and baby boomers. Millennials aren't joining, and boomers are discontinuing their membership. This has caused a major diminution in synagogue membership and negatively impacted synagogue income, in part because not all members pay the same rate of dues, and baby boomers who leave the synagogue are generally among those members paying the largest individual amounts in dues, since they have more discretionary income. As a result, synagogues usually need more than one new member to make up for one former member, since the new member is usually entering at a much lower dues rate than the member who resigned.

Finding Examples of Successful Innovations

Synagogue leaders look to a variety of sources for innovations. Among these sources are the megachurches, so called because of the sheer size of their membership. While there are certainly more

Christians than Jews in North America, synagogue leaders look to megachurches for guidance in welcoming newcomers and nurturing members in particular. Megachurches are able to maintain large memberships while attending to the needs of members as if these large churches were small, intimate institutions. As a result, the success of the megachurch is also driving some of the trends in synagogue renewal. Megachurches (such as the well-known Northpoint Community Church in Alpharetta, Georgia; Saddleback Church in Lake Forest, California; and Willow Creek Community Church in South Barrington, Illinois) do not charge dues. Yet they are able to raise the funds necessary to support their mission and vision.

Some synagogues that are experimenting with new practices that enhance their traditional membership-and-dues model deserve mention because they provide a foundation for eventual change to the entire membership and revenue model. For example, some synagogues are building sophisticated adult study back into their programming, such as the Skirball Center at Temple Emanu-El in New York City. Others, such as Congregation Or Zarua, are attempting to add a traditional *beit midrash* (open study space for sacred texts with instructors for guidance) into their programs.

Other synagogues are addressing solely economic issues. Anshe Emeth Memorial Temple, for example, a large Reform synagogue in New Brunswick, New Jersey, initiated a gift membership program

---

Anshe Emeth Gift Membership Program

Everyone loves being a part of Anshe Emeth. Give your friends an amazing gift—the gift of membership in our community! You can give your unaffiliated Jewish friends a one-year temple membership. Just call the temple office and ask for ... a Gift Membership Coupon. Present the coupon as your gift to your friends, and invite them to join you as a member of our community.

Anshe Emeth Memorial Temple (New Brunswick, New Jersey), "Gift Membership Program," *The Bulletin*, Summer 2014, www.aemt.net/about-us2/documents2/doc_download/387-summer-bulletin-2014.

---

to honor their 150th anniversary. Members in good standing were given the opportunity to provide an unaffiliated family with the gift of one year's free membership in the synagogue. Nearly forty-five gift memberships have been given over the past five years, and nearly thirty of those membership units are still affiliated with the institution. Since many of these members renewed their membership at the conclusion of their free year—the ultimate goal of the program and, according to its originators, its measure of success—the synagogue has continued the program.

As a way of handling their finances, Congregation Beth Adam, a humanistic congregation in Loveland, Ohio, approaches membership uniquely from the perspective of the individual rather than the family unit "to affirm clearly that singles are full and equal members of the congregation."[4] The annual membership fee is $825 for any adult in the household. (Two adults in the household would be $1650 and so on.) Children are free. Since, according to the synagogue, the base membership fees cover only about 50 percent of their operating expenses, "members who are able are asked to make an annual contribution to help close the gap between operating costs and revenue provided by base membership fees." Beth Adam also sponsors an online synagogue community called Our Jewish Community for which there is no charge.

Increasingly, synagogues are offering some segments of the potential member population a year of free or discounted membership. This reduction is often extended to individuals or couples under the age of thirty, especially those whose wedding was officiated by the rabbi of the synagogue. Temple Emanu-El of West Essex, a medium-size Reform synagogue in Livingston, New Jersey, no longer charges their preschool and day-care families any synagogue dues in addition to their school or day-care fees, and new members are able to set their own dues for the first two years (with a minimum of $600 per year). Emanu-El has changed their language as well, to refer to dues now as a "membership contribution." Congregation Beth Am (Reform) in Los Altos Hills, California, has a "36/36 Program," which allows anyone up to the age of thirty-six to belong to the synagogue for $36 per year. Temple Beit HaYam, a small Reform synagogue in Stuart, Florida, which adopted a voluntary dues program (explained in chapter 2), is quite explicit that "families with heads of household under 30 are asked to pay no more than $500, no questions asked."[5] The policy of Beth El Synagogue, a large Conservative synagogue in St. Louis Park, Minnesota, stipulates that for those thirty-three and under, married or single, without children, any donation or amount is welcome in exchange for membership. Similarly, Congregation B'nai Tzedek (Conservative) in Potomac, Maryland, recently offered new members a 25 percent discount off their first year of membership in honor of their twenty-fifth anniversary as a congregation. More recently, Congregation Beth Hatikvah, a small Reconstructionist synagogue in Summit, New Jersey, offered a "180 days for $180" option to allow families to try out the synagogue and the religious school. And of course, some synagogues—such as Temple Israel (Reform) in Memphis, Tennessee—have opened their doors for High Holy Day services to all, no tickets or fees required. Other institutions are partnering with their local Jewish Community Center in offering discounted memberships for those who join both institutions or offering one amount that entitles the individual or family to membership in both institutions. These programs and practices reflect an acknowledgment of the need to make changes to the membership and revenue models in the synagogue—the kind of changes that are described in the chapters ahead.

The Eternal One spoke to Moses, saying: Tell the Israelite people to bring Me gifts; you shall accept gifts for Me from every person whose heart is so moved.

Exodus 25:1–3

It is the challenge of spirituality—a direct connection to the Divine and an inspiring Judaism that moves us to contribute. It is the building of sacred community (*k'hilah k'doshah*) wherever that community gathers to study, pray, or do deeds of loving-kindness or *tikkun olam* to create a sacred space (*mikdash*).

Rabbi Peter S. Knobel[1]

2

Voluntary Dues

The model of voluntary dues, the first in our presentation of alternative approaches to synagogue membership and revenue, is sometimes called a freewill offering model. In this model, members are permitted to pay any amount to maintain their membership in the synagogue. Thus it honors all who pay into the system, regardless of the amount. In the voluntary dues model, synagogues determine their expenses, divide that amount by the number of membership units, and then tell members what their share is, leaving the ultimate decision about how much to contribute to each member. Thus, while the dues are indeed voluntary, the synagogue guides members by telling them how much it costs to operate the synagogue, so that they have a benchmark for their contribution. However, synagogue leaders provide no financial oversight. This model is sometimes called the sustaining model of synagogue membership, because members are told the real costs of maintaining the synagogue. The approach might seem contrary to the voluntary nature of the dues, but synagogues provide the information because people tend to think the synagogue's "products and services" cost far less than they do.

At Temple Beit HaYam in Stuart, Florida, the majority of members pledge at the sustaining level. But religious school tuition and building funds are not included in the voluntary dues program. As is the case in many Reform congregations, High Holy Day tickets are included in membership.

When Ohavi Zedek Synagogue, a Conservative synagogue in Burlington, Vermont, introduced a voluntary dues program in 2011

Membership at Temple Beit HaYam

Judaism is not a spectator sport. To be a Jew is to be part of a Jewish community that enriches our lives with joy and fulfillment. Membership at Temple Beit HaYam is an experience of lasting friendships, stimulating learning, meaningful worship, and the peace that comes with finding a spiritual home. Join Temple Beit HaYam and become part of a family. Temple Beit HaYam is one of a handful of congregations in the nation to scrap its dues system and replace it with a pledge system. Instead of paying an assigned fixed dues amount, our members pledge the amount they wish to contribute as their financial commitment. Each year, the Temple calculates the average level of giving needed to support our programs and services based on our operating budget. The majority of our members pledge at this sustaining level or higher. Those who are not able to pledge at the sustaining level strive to come as close as their finances will allow.

"Membership," Temple Beit HaYam website, www.tbhfl.org/become-a-member.html.

for their 400 member families, they recommended "3 percent of annual gross income" to members as a guideline for their voluntary pledge, although they encouraged members who "choose to belong as members and partners in community ... [to] each pledge support according to [their] belief in the organization and its mission."[2] Dues at Ohavi Zedek do not include High Holy Day tickets, religious school tuition, or the building fund.

When Temple Beth El, a medium-size Reform congregation in Aptos, California, introduced a voluntary dues model, they chose to use six categories to distinguish giving amounts—from the basic member at $36 and above, through pillar member at $10,500 and above. The sustaining membership is listed at $3,000 and above. High Holy Day tickets are included at Beth El, but religious school tuition and the building fund are extra costs for members.

The experience of those who have instituted a policy of voluntary dues is that the total amount of funds collected through a

Membership at Ohavi Zedek Synagogue

A synagogue membership is not something we buy, like membership at a gym. If we don't get to the gym regularly and use the services, there is no benefit of membership, so why pay the bill? A synagogue is much more than a membership organization; it is a congregational home, an extended family. Therefore we don't purchase synagogue membership with dues any longer, at least not here at OZ; we each choose to belong as members and partners in community, and we each pledge support according to our belief in the organization and its mission. Our annual membership pledges are an investment in the Jewish values, vision, and ideals that are the heart and soul of OZ.

"Ohavi Zedek Synagogue Membership Financial Support Guidelines 5774 (2013–2014)," Ohavi Zedek Synagogue website, http://ohavizedek.org/wp-content/uploads/2014/10/Ohavi-Zedek-Membership-Support-Guidelines-5774-2013-4.pdf.

voluntary system is generally consistent with what was collected prior to the policy change. It may even grow, as has been the case in some synagogues that have moved to the voluntary dues program. Since the budgets of most synagogues are not covered by dues (support ranges from 45 to 85 percent of the total operating budget), this system may still have to be augmented by other forms of fundraising if it is not designed to cover all of the synagogue's expenses.

The voluntary dues model does indeed have more potential to cover a larger portion of the operating costs of the synagogue than does the traditional dues model. When synagogue leaders share with members the total expenses of the synagogue and specify members' share, they invite the possibility of covering the entire operating budget through voluntary giving. Through this model, leaders are also more willing to develop budgets that presume that member dues will cover all of the expenses of the synagogue. Even when the amount of suggested dues in the voluntary system is the same as the previously assessed amount, potential members are attracted to the synagogue because perceived cost barriers are lowered.

Becoming a Member

Temple Beth El is a covenantal congregation of members who support each other, the larger community, and are committed to the continuity of Jewish life in Santa Cruz. Every member is asked to make a financial contribution that reflects the particular capabilities of their household in order to continue to build and sustain our community.... We appreciate you giving as much as you can.

Formal Definition of Membership at Temple Beth El

Section 1. Qualification for General Membership

The following two conditions are prerequisites for Temple membership:

(a) Any person who resides in Santa Cruz, Santa Clara, Monterey or San Benito Counties, and meets one of these criteria:

- (i) a person who is Jewish by birth, either through matrilineal or patrilineal descent, or conversion;
- (ii) a person who is not Jewish but supports the Jewish beliefs, practices, and Temple involvement of their Jewish spouse, committed partner, or children;
- (iii) a person, regardless of faith, who was previously part of a Temple member family unit and now agrees to support Jewish beliefs and practices and the mission of Temple Beth El;
- (iv) a person who is a continuing Temple member at the time these criteria are adopted....

(b) Maintenance of membership status requires payment of dues in accordance with the policies of the Board of Directors.

"Becoming a Member," Temple Beth El website, https://tbeaptos.org/civicrm/contribute/transact?reset=1&id=63. Bylaws on qualifications for membership can be found at https://tbeaptos.org/sites/default/files/images/2013%20TBE%20Bylaws.pdf.

Voluntary dues are different from the fair share model (which may be considered a form of progressive tax) used by the Union for Reform Judaism, which sets dues as a percentage of the individual's income (calculated voluntarily by the individual member). Large synagogues such as Congregation Beth Israel (Reform) in Houston, Texas, use the fair share model, and dues income makes up 80 percent of the annual budget. At Beth Israel, all members in good standing receive High Holy Day tickets and have voting rights in the synagogue. There is no building fund requirement and the synagogue is working to build their endowment with the goal of reducing dependence on dues. Other organizations use the term "fair share" to refer to flat dues (the same amount per household).

Of all of the new methods being introduced into the North American synagogue for the collection of revenue, the system of voluntary dues is by far the most popular, even for those synagogues that are the most risk averse. About thirty congregations, the majority of them affiliated with the Union for Reform Judaism, have adopted a voluntary dues model. Some synagogues, like Beth Chaim Congregation in Danville, California, which is not affiliated with any of the Jewish religious movements, experimented first with a no-dues policy before moving to a voluntary dues approach. Beth Chaim's rabbi, Dan Goldblatt, announced the change during High Holy Day services, when ostensibly the entire congregation is in attendance. Other congregations, like Anshe Chesed/ Fairmount Temple in Cleveland, Ohio, a large Reform congregation, offer voluntary dues to first-year members only. At Fairmount Temple, these first-year members are still responsible for the building fund ($1,500 payable over five years), and they have voting rights like all other members.

With Rabbi Scott Hausman-Weiss at the helm, the practice of the recently founded Congregation Shma Koleinu in Bellaire, Texas, is to provide members with the entire cost of operating the synagogue, divided by the number of family units who have chosen to affiliate with the congregation. That amount, per family unit, thereby becomes the baseline or standard contribution. But members still determine if that's what they want to pay. From the inception of the synagogue, Hausman-Weiss's goal has been for the voluntary dues plan to cover nearly all of the operating expenses of the synagogue.

Help Us Build This Sacred Assembly

Our hope is that households that choose to contribute to [Congregation Shma Koleinu] will give enough to cover our average cost of $200 per month per household. This level of support will allow us to continue to offer the services and programming our community has enjoyed since its inception just ten months ago. We invite you to become a monthly supporter of CSK and know that when you do, your donation makes it possible for all of us to continue building our sacred community. If our financial goal of $200 per month fits into your budget, that is wonderful. If it is a bit larger than your budget, your monthly contribution at any level means the world to us. And if your budget is quite a bit larger, we invite you to help us ensure that CSK is available to all who seek us out.

From the Bylaws: Eligible Voting Participants

Congregants may elect to participate in all religious, educational, charitable and other programming of Congregation Shma Koleinu, but choose not to vote on matters presented to the congregation. To vote on matters presented to the congregation, a congregant must be admitted as a "Voting Participant" of Congregation Shma Koleinu. Anyone of the Jewish faith, 18 years of age or older ("adult"), may apply to be a Voting Participant. The Leadership Team shall adopt, and may amend, a form to apply to be a Voting Participant. At the next regular meeting of the Leadership Team after submission of an application to be a Voting Participant, the Leadership Team shall meet to consider such application and either vote to admit the applicant as a Voting Participant or deny membership as a Voting Participant. After June 18, 2014, a Voting Participant may not vote at any meeting of Congregation Shma Koleinu until ninety (90) days have passed after admission as a Voting Participant.

Any family of at least one Jewish spouse or any household with at least one Jewish person may apply to be a Voting Participant. Once admitted as a Voting Participant, each adult member of that family or household shall be considered an individual Voting Participant of Congregation Shma Koleinu so long as they are members in good standing. Good standing shall mean that all financial obligations to Congregation Shma Koleinu are current.

Adults seeking to convert and their households shall be invited to participate in all religious, educational, charitable and other programming of Congregation Shma Koleinu, but shall not be entitled to be a Voting Participant until the Senior Rabbi has certified at least one adult's conversion to the Jewish faith.

"Monthly Contribution," Congregation Shma Koleinu website, www.shmakoleinu.com/?page_id=1603. Bylaws on qualifications for membership can be found at www.shmakoleinu.com/wp-content/uploads/2014/01/CSK_Bylaws_061514.pdf.

Congregation Sukkat Shalom

Wilmette, Illinois ▣ Reform ▣ Small

We can learn from the example of other synagogues that have adopted a voluntary dues system. Congregation Sukkat Shalom was founded twenty years ago, although their origins can be traced to a small group of intermarried couples who had been meeting for support and education for five or six years prior to the founding of the congregation. In establishing the congregation, basic assumptions of synagogue life were questioned. First, the synagogue always fully embraced the diversity of their members' backgrounds, including spouses, partners, and parents who came from religions-of-origin other than Judaism. Sukkat Shalom wanted to offer meaningful spiritual experiences for all. While fully within Jewish tradition, the language, music, learning, and liturgy of the synagogue were always shaped to send a message of welcome to all.

From their inception, the community designed their programs to both accommodate and address their fundamental diversity. So that family members from traditions other than Judaism could learn about the faith, education was not focused on the individual student but was always family based.

At the same time, some financial practices familiar to Jewish family members were rejected. For example, the idea of "dues" or "tickets" for High Holy Day worship was foreign—and even offensive—to those raised in other faiths. Many Jews also objected to that system. As a result, the synagogue's leaders redefined the congregation and began to refer to themselves as a donor-based faith community, that is, a synagogue solely supported by voluntary giving. People were asked to make an annual pledge. In the first year or two of the congregation's existence, the amount of the pledge was left totally to the discretion of the member. A pledge card was later developed that listed specific giving levels, but categories of giving were not based on age or marital status. Membership in the synagogue was open to people who gave less than the suggested amount. One did not have to request an adjustment in dues. All giving was voluntary and confidential—with no committee review or oversight.

According to Rabbi Sam Gordon, Sukkat Shalom's spiritual leader and founding rabbi, this system was far more consistent with church giving in response to stewardship campaigns. Annual commitments were made, and all understood that *tzedekah* (charitable giving) was the driving value behind dues. Even when the congregation purchased and renovated their building, the capital giving campaign invited members to make voluntary contributions. Many chose to make five-year pledges. There was no published list of donors. There were no naming opportunities, no donor plaques. Only the executive director and bookkeeper knew the size of donors' gifts. This approach broke from contemporary Jewish giving patterns and expectations. For the leaders, recognizing that the long accepted Jewish vocabulary of synagogue life can be off-putting to new entrants into the Jewish world is crucial. Sukkat Shalom's leaders believed they had to implement broad institutional change to truly transform the atmosphere into one of welcome and acceptance.

Temple Israel

Sharon, Massachusetts ▣ Conservative ▣ Medium

Temple Israel was an early adopter of the voluntary dues system in 2008. Their leaders realized that they were regularly raising dues to meet the growing demands of their budget. Rather than increasing total income, however, raising dues was actually causing the synagogue to lose revenue. Members made the choice to disaffiliate rather than pay higher synagogue dues. Temple Israel leaders considered—but did not adopt—a fair share dues policy based on a percentage of individuals' income. Once Temple Israel implemented a voluntary dues policy, synagogue leaders saw their income initially decline but not as fast as it had when they raised dues. Three years later, the trend was reversed, and total income was up 4 percent. And then the synagogue saw an increase in membership as well. By their actions, people were affirming the new approach to dues and membership. Moreover, the synagogue did not have to chase after anyone to collect their dues, since giving was entirely voluntary. Members actually paid higher amounts in the voluntary system than they had when they were assessed a specific amount. Nonetheless, the synagogue did experience a decline in their High Holy Day appeal once the voluntary dues system was put into place.

Temple Israel refers to the desired level of giving as an annual commitment level or sustaining level. If each member pays this portion of the annual operating expenses, the synagogue stays fiscally solvent. Since the synagogue allows people to pay according to their means, however, leaders also need to conduct more traditional fundraising activities. In addition, while the voluntary dues at Temple Israel include High Holy Day tickets as a member benefit, religious school tuition fees and required building fund contributions for new members (paid out over six years) are mandatory.

Temple Beth Tzedek

Amherst, New York ▣ Conservative ▣ Medium

Other synagogues that have implemented a voluntary dues system demonstrate possible adaptations. Temple Beth El merged with Temple Shaarey Zedek in 2008 to become Temple Beth Tzedek. Subsequently, the merged synagogue established a voluntary dues program. The synagogue's website cites Temple Israel's program as motivation for the adoption of a program of their own. In their own variation on Temple Israel's system, those who do not submit their pledge forms are billed at 3 percent higher than their previous pledge. This practice encourages pledging and makes financial planning easier for synagogue leaders. There is no building fund charge. While religious school tuition is not included in dues, members get a reduced rate. High Holy Day tickets are included. All members in good standing are eligible to vote.

Temple Kol Ami

West Bloomfield, Michigan ▣ Reform ▣ Small

Temple Kol Ami (TKA) also followed the lead of Temple Israel and was among the early adopters of a similar voluntary dues system. TKA calls their system T'rumot HaLev (Gifts of the Heart), which they consider a pledge system. Ironically, TKA's pledge system is very similar to what was the prevailing system among churches for collecting funds when synagogues originally adopted the membership dues system. At TKA, members are asked to make an annual pledge, from which the annual budget for the synagogue is shaped. The synagogue provides members with a recommended target range for such pledges. High Holy Day tickets are included. However, members are still required to pay other standard fees, such as religious school tuition and bar/bat mitzvah fees, and to make a commitment to the building fund. TKA has limited membership to 500 families, according to the membership brochure, "to ensure that Temple Kol Ami remains a warm and welcoming place to gather ... small enough to offer a personal touch; large enough to offer a wide variety of social and educational programming." Because they have a cap on membership, TKA thus shares some of the attributes of a boutique synagogue, as described in the concluding chapter of this book.

Temple Brith Achim

King of Prussia, Pennsylvania ▣ Reform ▣ Small

Making the transition to a voluntary dues program in 2011, Temple Brith Achim encourages both "gifts of the heart and gifts of the hand,"[3] emphasizing the need for both financial and human resources in order for the congregation to be sustained. It is the acknowledgment that a change in the revenue structure is insufficient to sustain the synagogue that makes Brith Achim's approach to voluntary giving an important contribution to the conversation about a change in membership and revenue models. At Brith Achim, High Holy Day tickets are included with dues, but members are still required to pay religious school tuition and support the building fund. Of the 275 membership units in the congregation, Brith Achim notes that about 50 percent of their members are intermarried, about 15 percent higher than the national average for Reform synagogues. Like Sukkat Shalom, it is quite probable that the congregational makeup of Brith Achim makes their members more receptive to a program of voluntary giving.

Congregation Or Shalom

Berwyn, Pennsylvania ▣ Conservative ▣ Small

Not far from Brith Achim, Congregation Or Shalom, a synagogue about forty years old, also introduced a voluntary giving program, telling their members to "pledge what you can afford." However, they categorize members' giving in the following groups: Bronze, Silver, Gold, and Platinum. Clearly, though, one congregation's transition to a voluntary dues program encourages other congregations in the community to follow their example.

Tifereth Israel Synagogue

San Carlos, California ▣ Conservative ▣ Small

Leaders at Tifereth Israel Synagogue, founded in 1905 in the San Diego area, have named their new voluntary dues program T'rumah, drawing on the Hebrew term for the "elevation offering." According to the synagogue website, "We believe that membership should reflect a relationship and experience within our *kehillah* (community). Membership is voluntary and we invite you to contribute as 'your heart so moves you' and [this] should reflect your personal commitment to our congregation."[4] Furthermore, the synagogue shares their annual operating expenses with the entire congregation so that congregants can determine their contribution for the coming year, which will include their High Holy Day pledge. Of course, say the congregation's leaders, the sustaining number may change annually due to a variety of factors. The synagogue also established four levels of giving beyond the sustaining amount to recognize donors: Sustainer, Builder, Pillar, and Cornerstone. They also welcome donations commemorating life-cycle events and are committed to continue ongoing fundraising events. High Holy Day tickets are included in membership, but religious school tuition fees are additional. Members enjoy full voting rights at the synagogue, and there is no building fund obligation.

Temple B'nai Or

Morristown, New Jersey ▣ Reform ▣ Medium

A recent adopter of the voluntary dues program, Temple B'nai Or calls their program Kehilah (community). They ask each member family to make both a voluntary financial commitment and a pledge to volunteer. According to the synagogue website, "Both are determined by Temple costs and needs, not member age or income. Each year in June, Temple members fill out and return their Kehilah forms with their renewed pledges for the new fiscal year." Unlike other synagogues that are focused on the financial pledge, B'nai Or has tied finances to program. "The volunteer pledge form creates a resource of the skills and interests within the congregation. It is just as critical as the Voluntary Financial Commitment."[5]

Synagogue leaders at B'nai Or suggest a sustaining pledge, which is based on the amount needed from every adult member to maintain the synagogue, including facilities, programs, and staff. Members are reminded that those who want to make higher pledges to the synagogue are welcome to do so. In addition, those who cannot meet the sustaining amount are told to "fill in what they can give, no questions asked."[6] Religious school tuition is not included in annual membership dues at B'nai Or. There is no building fund, and High Holy Day tickets are included with membership dues. All members have voting rights at the synagogue.

Membership at Temple B'nai Or

At Temple B'nai Or, we strive to enable families to join with us and stay with us for generations. Our membership program adopts the emerging model that eliminates traditional dues and instead asks members for a voluntary financial commitment and a volunteer pledge. We call it *Kehilah*—Hebrew for community—to signify the importance of each member's role and responsibility to each other and our traditions. We now ask our members to contribute financially and by participating in Temple life based on the needs of the Kehilah, not based on age or income. Together, we make a commitment to sustain Temple B'nai Or.

"Become a Member of Our Community," Temple B'nai Or website, http://templebnaior.org/join/become-a-member/.

Temple Emanu-El

Marblehead, Massachusetts ▣ Reform ▣ Medium

Adopting the voluntary system in 2014, Temple Emanu-El considers a member anyone who makes a pledge of any amount. Membership includes voting rights in the synagogue, as well as High Holy Day tickets. Members are also obligated to contribute to the building fund, and families who send their children to religious school are charged tuition fees. The change to the voluntary model was a response to synagogue leaders' sense over the preceding few years that they were heading toward a fee-for-service model, which they assiduously wanted to avoid. (The synagogue had seen a decline in membership from about 600 family units to under 500.) Synagogue leaders felt that moving toward a fee-for-service model would undermine the essential nature of the synagogue community. David J. Meyer, Emanu-El's rabbi, suggests that his congregation values relationships over membership in this statement on the synagogue's website: "We are, first and foremost, a community that emphasizes relationships even more than programming, belonging even more than membership, and a place where Jewish life is not 'consumed,' but created!"[7] Like some other congregations, Temple Emanu-El recognizes those who give beyond the sustaining level.

Congregation Beth Am

Buffalo Grove, Illinois ▣ Reform ▣ Small

Calling their system the Affordable Membership Initiative, Congregation Beth Am made the decision for the 2014–2015 fiscal year to permit members to assess their own dues, offering guidance from the fair share concept that members give 1.5 to 2.4 percent of their annual income. Members are encouraged to make any adjustments necessary, given any current personal financial challenges. There is no board oversight. While there is a flat fee for religious school tuition charged per student, previously required building fund contributions are no longer assessed, and previous discounts for

---

Congregation Beth Am New Dues Structure 2014–2015: Frequently Asked Questions

1. What is the goal of the initiative?

The aim is to increase the number of Beth Am members by putting into place a dues structure which is affordable to all who may be interested in joining, including those with lower incomes who may not have been able to consider temple membership in the past.

2. Why is this being put into place now?

At Beth Am's current membership size, there is little chance that Beth Am will be able to afford to both keep their current programs intact and at the same time recentralize their worship and office operations into a single space. A paradigm shift will be required to achieve both, and this initiative is designed to provide that new paradigm.

"Congregation Beth Am New Dues Structure 2014–2015," Congregation Beth Am website, www.congregation-betham.org/_data/docs/14-15%20cba%20affordable%20membership%20initiative.pdf.

---

demographic groups such as singles and older adults have been eliminated. High Holy Day tickets are included with membership. The synagogue's goal is simple: "The aim is to increase the number of Beth Am members by putting into place a dues structure which is affordable to all who may be interested in joining, including those with lower incomes who may not have been able to consider temple membership in the past."[8]

Congregation Bet Shalom

Tucson, Arizona ▣ Conservative ▣ Small

Congregation Bet Shalom recently made the switch to a "free-will, pay-what-you-like policy." Congregants register for membership online and are greeted with this notice: "Congregation Bet Shalom does not require dues for membership!" While contributions are encouraged, religious school education is free for kindergarten and first grade. Tuition is charged for second grade and up. The synagogue began offering High Holy Day tickets for free, which unexpectedly yielded larger donations to the synagogue. Recognizing the various configurations of a Jewish family today, Congregation Bet Shalom offers an "unaffiliated partner" option, which is clarified with the following instruction: "Spouses: non-Jewish or not interested in membership. A contribution pledge to Congregation Bet Shalom may be made by an unaffiliated partner."[9] Only members have voting rights in the synagogue.

Panera Cares

Synagogues are not alone in experimenting with a voluntary system of payment. Panera Cares, a program of Panera Bread bakeries and cafes, is one of several for-profit enterprises that uses a voluntary payment system in a limited number of its restaurants. The intent is that those who can afford to pay for their meals will also pay for those who are unable to do so. Suggested donations are listed for the meals, but there are no specific requirements. Those unable to contribute funds to support the meals of others can also volunteer to work.

Panera took its lead from the nonprofit model One World Everybody Eats, the first pay-as-you-can cafe in North America, established by Denise Cerreta in Salt Lake City in 2003. While other cafes remain open, the original cafe closed in 2012—but not before spawning numerous others throughout the country that followed the same voluntary payment model.

Highlights

The voluntary dues model has been adopted by more synagogues than any of the other new models presented in this book. Thus, there is more empirical evidence to help leaders determine whether it is the right fit for a particular synagogue.

1. In a voluntary dues system, the membership model doesn't change, but there is no financial oversight in the determining of individual dues.
2. The specific amount of dues to be paid is determined by the individual member, although synagogues may make suggestions to the members based on the operating costs of the synagogue.
3. Since dues—either required or voluntary—generally do not cover the entirety of the synagogue's budget, other fundraising may still be required.

Frequently Asked Questions

Critics of the voluntary dues model may be fearful that if people are given the choice, they will choose not to pay anything for synagogue dues—or pay a lesser amount than is needed for the synagogue to operate. Institutions—both religious and secular—that have instituted a voluntary dues or payment program have found that this is not the case. When people value what an institution has to offer, they are willing to pay for it. That is why synagogues must make explicit to members the personal benefit of their offerings. Of course, a tiny minority of people may not voluntarily contribute. They should be welcomed as members nonetheless.

Can a member choose not to pay anything?

Yes. Nevertheless, while the amount of dues paid is voluntary, members should be encouraged to pay even a small amount.

How does the individual member determine what to pay as dues?

Some synagogues provide no guidance to help members determine the amount of voluntary dues. Other synagogues tell members the real costs per membership unit (dividing the annual budget by the number of members), so that members know what their share of the cost is.

Why is this model so prevalent?

This model is prevalent for three reasons. First, it was adopted earlier than most of the other models described in this book. Second, it seems to have the least amount of risk. Third, it is client centered rather than institutionally focused, acknowledging individuals' need to understand where they fit into the synagogue enterprise.

Implementation Steps

Step 1. Determine the sustainable annual contribution of a membership unit by dividing your total budget by the total number of member households. This information should be shared with members as the "sustaining amount" for membership.

Step 2. Communicate with your community why the change to voluntary giving was made, as well as the leaders' desire to use voluntary dues to meet the operating expenses of the synagogue so additional fundraising will not be necessary.

Step 3. Develop a contingency plan for supplemental revenue, especially to underwrite any potential budget deficit in the first year of the new model's implementation.

Step 4. Develop and roll out marketing materials that reflect the new membership model.

Notes for Adapting This Model for Our Synagogue

Israel lives in its congregations.

Rabbi Isaac Mayer Wise[1]

We reconceptualized synagogue membership as a sacred contract with a community, where our gifts and our passions are recognized, nourished, and directed toward the enrichment of others.

Rabbi Lawrence A. Hoffman[2]

3

No Dues or "Gifts of the Heart"

While many people will read this book because it addresses the finances of the synagogue, this chapter is about synagogues whose visionary leaders believe that the notion of "no dues" is a religious principle rather than an economic practice—that we should open the doors of our synagogues to anyone who wants to enter, without any financial barrier. The no-dues model is about equal access to the synagogue for everyone, plain and simple. It is about eliminating the so-called pay-to-pray posture that North American synagogues have assumed in their efforts to grapple with real financial challenges. Some naysayers suggest that people value only what they pay for. Proponents argue that more people will try out the synagogue and its program offerings if there is no financial downside to doing so and that if they have a positive, soul-enriching experience, they may return and eventually support the institution.

Some congregations see the work of neighboring no-dues synagogues as an attempt to financially undermine their own congregations. Some congregations may simply cut their fees to attract members in what they see as a competitive marketplace; others may be committed philosophically to a no-dues model.

While some synagogues have arrived at a no-dues policy through a series of stages—often from mandatory dues to voluntary dues and then no dues—other synagogues have been founded on a philosophy of no dues, even if the notion of membership itself has not changed. Such is the case with the Woodstock (Vermont) Area Jewish Community/Congregation Shir Shalom (described below).

Purposes of the Woodstock Area Jewish Community/Congregation Shir Shalom

The Woodstock Area Jewish Community (WAJC), Inc., has been formed for the following purposes:

1. To promote and facilitate an appreciation for and the practice of Judaism in all of its cultural and religious aspects in central Vermont.
2. To provide a forum for Jewish worship, education, and cultural and social activities for people of all ages and backgrounds.
3. To raise funds, disseminate information, and, in general, to do all other acts and things incidental to and in furtherance of the aforesaid purposes.
4. To exercise all other powers conferred upon charitable religious corporations by the laws of the State of Vermont.

From the amended bylaws as approved at the special meeting of the Woodstock Area Jewish Community, Inc., September 15, 2006.

Other synagogues have made the reverse journey, however. Stephen Wise Free Synagogue in New York City was founded in 1907 as a no-dues synagogue ("free" in the synagogue's name referred to a variety of things, including freedom of speech from the pulpit, at the time of their founding) before they introduced a traditional dues system, which they still maintain.

The no-dues model is quite different from the no-membership model discussed in chapter 6. "No dues" means the institution has members but they are not obligated to contribute any synagogue dues. A variation on the no-dues model is the sponsorship model, where participation in a synagogue program is underwritten by a sponsor. For example, someone without school-age kids might subsidize a program of religious education designed for families who can't afford a Jewish education for their children, because they believe in the value of such an education. Some of these programs operate independently from the synagogue. One example of the sponsorship model is the Stepping Stones program at Temple

Emanuel in Denver, Colorado. Stepping Stones is a free religious school for intermarried families and their children, sponsored by individual donors and attached to the synagogue.

Woodstock Area Jewish Community/Congregation Shir Shalom

Woodstock, Vermont ▣ Reform ▣ Small

The Woodstock Area Jewish Community/Congregation Shir Shalom in Woodstock, Vermont, was established over twenty-five years ago to reach Jews and their families in the area. In their bylaws, they first established the purposes of the congregation.

The bylaws then provided that "any person of the Jewish faith 13 years of age or over, or any person 18 years of age or older, who has demonstrated a commitment to one or more of the purposes of the Congregation and seeks to be associated with the Congregation, may elect to become a member.... Each member shall have one vote on matters coming before meetings of the Congregation." Since the synagogue's inception, there has never been a required building fund, religious school tuition, or fees for High Holy Day seats. It is important to note that the no-dues model was never a financial planning strategy. The synagogue's approach was a reaction to the prevailing pay-to-pray model, according to Stuart M. Matlins, who founded the congregation along with his wife, Antoinette, and who was the spiritual leader for nineteen years. In eliminating all barriers to participation, including perhaps the most formidable—the financial barrier—the congregation was able to welcome all who sought to express their Jewish identity in rural central Vermont. While the congregation encountered skeptics along the way, the vision-driven strategy served the congregation well as they purchased a building, built a 250-seat sanctuary, and sustained a religious school for 40 to 50 children, and it now provides the financial resources for rabbinic and educational leaders.

How is this model sustained? According to Matlins, "We serve people. We never ask them individually for money." This emerges from Matlins's philosophy that there are two ways to interact with people in organizations—either through control or through service. Since a synagogue can't really exercise any control over people in a liberal world, particularly in areas of low Jewish population where there is no social pressure to lead any part of a Jewish life, all they can do is serve their potential target population. From the voluntary response of individuals to high-quality service, the synagogue is able to thrive. For Matlins, synagogue leaders need to ask three questions *in this order* (not in the reverse order, as most leaders do):

1. Is it the right thing to do?
2. Who will do it?
3. How do we pay for it?

"The money will always be found," contends Matlins, who has been correct for a quarter of a century.

The New Shul

Scottsdale, Arizona ▣ Independent ▣ Small

The New Shul was founded in 2002 and is led by a husband-and-wife team of rabbis, Michael Wasserman and Elana Kanter, both ordained by The Jewish Theological Seminary. According to the congregation's philosophy, "At The New Shul, there are no membership dues. Instead we rely on voluntary support by our members to sustain ourselves financially. We charge no dues in order to emphasize that membership in a spiritual community is not something that one can

---

Membership at The New Shul

If you don't charge dues, how do you pay the bills?

We never tell anyone how much to give, but we do depend on everyone to do their part. Each year, before Rosh Hashanah, we send out a letter to all of our members explaining how much it will cost to run the shul for the coming year, and asking everyone to tell us what they think they can contribute. Everyone pledges what they can, and somehow we always manage. We should add that we keep our expenses to a bare minimum to make it easier for everyone.

"Frequently Asked Questions," The New Shul website, http://thenewshul.org/faqs/.

---

buy. Financial support is not the cost of belonging, but an expression of belonging. Our membership form offers some suggested amounts."[3] There is no charge for High Holy Day seats, member or not. There is also no building fund assessment of The New Shul's members. While there is no religious school at this synagogue, The New Shul does offer an alternative in the form of family classes, for which there is no charge. Voting rights among membership is handled in a unique way. According to Rabbi Michael Wasserman, the synagogue has a board, which is called a steering committee. Members of this steering committee have staggered two-year terms, and the committee chooses their own successors. This committee operates by consensus, as does the entire synagogue. There is an annual shul-wide meeting—and other meetings as needed—to discuss any large issues confronting the congregation, but there are no formal votes taken.[4]

Mitziut

Chicago, Illinois ▣ Independent ▣ Small

Located in the Rogers Park section of Chicago, Mitziut describes itself in a variety of ways to establish that it is an alternative institution: independent, nondenominational, spiritual, safe, non-judgmental, take-off-your-shoes-if-you-like, diverse. Mitziut's goal is that those who gather for worship should consider themselves as a synagogue community. One can certainly join Mitziut as a member, but according to the website, "The only requirement of membership is providing information on the Mitziut Membership Form and agreeing with the Mitziut values."[5] Consistent with their identity as an alternative synagogue, Mitziut leaders do not require members and participants to pay dues but do encourage them to give time, in-kind donations, or money to the community. As a corollary to these giving options, Mitziut is careful to point out, "There are no minimum requirements for any category, however, ... suggestions [of specific amounts] were established to help members in their decision making."[6] Because Mitziut sees membership as driven by the individual rather than the institution ("Membership in Mitziut is wanting to be a member of a community and wanting to help bring the vision to actuality"[7]), the notion of dues is irrelevant. People give because they feel loyalty to the institution, rather than because the institution requires them to do so.

Highlights

Dues, the collection of dues, and everything else related to dues consume a great deal of synagogues' human resources. Since this model does not require any dues, these resources can be directed toward other activities, including fundraising among those who can afford it, perhaps in the form of "relationship fundraising," an approach that puts the relationship with the donor first. Since there are no dues, potential members with a variety of talents may be attracted to the institution.

1. A no-dues synagogue charges no dues to members. Funds are raised through voluntary giving by those motivated to do so, as well as by relationship fundraising among those individuals who are capable of making significant contributions to the synagogue.
2. Some synagogues evolve into a no-dues policy. Others build no dues into their foundational philosophy.

Frequently Asked Questions

The biggest pushback against a no-dues model will undoubtedly come from those who fear that the synagogue will lose its primary revenue stream without dues-paying members—and the fear that someone will be getting a free ride. Leaders considering this model should share with these critics the dues and membership patterns in the congregation if the synagogue has experienced membership decline following dues increases. Leaders should also educate objectors about the increasing disdain that people feel toward the requirement to pay dues and the often invasive process of financial oversight of some synagogues.

Finally, synagogue leaders should share examples of successful institutions that have implemented a no-dues model.

How can the synagogue sustain itself without dues?

There are a variety of approaches to the collection of revenue in synagogues. Dues represent only one of these approaches. For example, financial support can also be gained through general fundraising appeals and targeted fundraising from specific individuals who have the capacity to support the congregation. However, a broadly based financial response, rather than reliance on a few generous people, may surprise congregational leaders and members with its success.

Why would people be motivated to financially support an institution if such support is not required to become a member?

Synagogues can only expect such support primarily from engaged members. Thus, the focus should be on developing programs and strategies that engage, educate, and spiritually inspire people and that are designed specifically to meet the needs of members, rather than the needs of the synagogue.

Implementation Steps

Step 1. Since no dues will be charged to members, the most important step will be creating an inspiring mission and programs and a financial resource development plan to replace the dues that will no longer be collected. One way to determine the revenue required by the synagogue is to evaluate the membership data of the synagogue. Determine what percentage of the membership contributes what percentage of income. Divide your membership into segments based on the level of their contribution to synagogue revenue. Then specify in your plan the income that needs to be raised from these population segments.

Step 2. Develop an engagement plan for each population segment whose dues are to be eliminated. Begin the transition to the new model by eliminating dues for the population segment that provides the least amount of financial support to the synagogue.

Notes for Adapting This Model for Our Synagogue

Whoever establishes for oneself a place to pray will receive the help of the God of Abraham [and Sarah].

Babylonian Talmud, *Berakhot* 8a

Only here, only in a synagogue, is the unique and infinite divinity of every human being brought into full relief in a communal context. One can go to the Grand Canyon to feel God's presence; one can, according to Jewish law, pray pretty much wherever one pleases. But only here, only in a synagogue, can you be part of a community whose operating assumption is that everyone—young and old, rich and poor, single and married, people you like and don't like—all of us exist equally, collectively and covenantally in God's image and presence. With each birth, a new world begins that never existed before. With each death, we lose a life that can never be replaced. In sin, we arrive here knowing that despite our shortcomings, we may still seek spiritual rehabilitation and repair; our flaws do not preclude us from standing before God or our fellow humanity. Just the opposite, in this place we are reminded that God's presence dwells within sinner and saint alike. In our joy we come here to express our thanksgiving to God.... And in our sorrow, we come here to ponder the burdensome mystery of a world in which inexplicable pain exists. If God's presence is elusive, then a synagogue bears the promise that another person may brighten our darkness by way of the light of their divine spark, and together we may mend a broken world.

Rabbi Elliot J. Cosgrove[1]

4

Transactional Membership

The transactional model is sometimes called the fee-for-service model, because people are charged only for the synagogue services they use. In the transactional model, participants become clients of the institution or its professional leaders, much like they become patients of a physician they see regularly or clients of an accountant they use annually to assist with income taxes and other financial matters. Lisa Harris Glass of the Synagogue Leadership Initiative, a project of the Jewish Federation of Northern New Jersey, refers to the transactional model as the tapas model, since members pay separately for different services in much the same way one might choose small servings of different dishes in a Spanish tapas restaurant. There the variety of small portions attracts customers and motivates them to cross the threshold of the restaurant in the first place.

The fee-for-service model is already in place in synagogues that employ a traditional membership model. We just don't fully acknowledge it. In the traditional membership model, members are provided with certain basic services. Because they already have a membership relationship with the synagogue, they are also entitled to pay for specific additional services that are not available to nonmembers, such as High Holy Day seats, religious school tuition, or *b'nai mitzvah* fees and the like. In most cases, if membership dues are not up to date, then members are not permitted to take advantage of these additional services.

Furthermore, a subculture that operates on a fee-for-service basis and is often sanctioned—even arranged—by the synagogue already exists outside of the synagogue in the Jewish community. *B'nai mitz-*

vah tutors and others in the community who possess particular skills are used by synagogues and paid by members for additional services not provided by the synagogue. Nonetheless, the services offered by these individuals may be required for participation in the synagogue. For example, synagogues may sponsor potential Jews-by-choice and require candidates for conversion to take an introduction to Judaism course, but not provide a program for them. These courses, like *b'nai mitzvah* tutoring, are often outsourced, and the candidates for conversion are required to pay for these services.

Many of us have experience in other realms of our life switching from all-inclusive membership dues to a fee-for-service model. For example, while golf courses used to be exclusively reserved for members and their guests, many golf courses now make themselves available to the general public on a fee-for-service basis. Such is the case with the Bunker Hill Golf Course in Princeton, New Jersey, which is available to anyone who wants to pay its green fee to play the course. Some golf courses offer various services beyond green fees, such as cart rentals and professional instruction, which can be purchased individually without the need for membership in the golf course. Other golf courses sponsor additional sports activities, as well as dining facilities—all of which are available for a fee.

One of the challenges in shifting to the transactional model is that the Jewish community is not used to an explicit fee-for-service approach, so synagogues might have difficulty determining what price the local market will bear for the services offered. Based on their experience with current membership models in place in synagogues, people may be willing to pay for obvious things like Jewish education and life-cycle events, for example. They may also be willing to pay for tickets to High Holy Day services. But potential clients may have to be persuaded to pay for other services for which they are unaccustomed to paying, such as counseling by clergy or hospital and home visits—services that have been included in a general membership without being itemized. Synagogues might also have difficulty determining how to cost out the services provided by the congregation or professional staff that are usually available to members under the traditional dues model. One option might be for members who want general access to the professional staff to pay a retainer.

People have a variety of objections to the transactional membership approach. Some find the notion of explicit fee-for-service in the synagogue simply distasteful. It places the rabbi and other synagogue clergy in the same category as secular service providers and may undermine the sacred nature of their relationship with synagogue members. This distaste may just be a result of their lack of familiarity with this model in the Jewish community. Others argue that it undermines the notion of community and its importance, since in a fee-for-service model, individuals relate to the institution as consumers, as they do in other aspects of their lives, rather than as members of a community where they support one another. Some people contend that synagogues that adopt the transactional model have fallen victim to current consumer trends in American culture, trends synagogues should be bucking, because the synagogue upholds values that are often counter to prevailing societal values.

Some people might also object that the transactional model creates an undesirable and even awkward relationship between client members and the synagogue, because the relationship becomes centered on the payment of a fee for a particular service and is not about the relationship that might be established between people in the context of community. In other words, it becomes all about the money. Yet people generally expect to develop relationships with those who provide them with professional services and at the same time to pay for the services the professionals render. A financial arrangement does not impede their relationship with service providers. Why should we presume that paying for specific services would necessarily damage our relationship with the synagogue or its clergy?

Tamid: The Downtown Synagogue

New York City ▣ Reform ▣ Small

A relative newcomer to New York's organized Jewish community, Tamid was founded in 2012 by Rabbi Darren Levine to serve progressive Jews in downtown Manhattan. In addition to worship services, Tamid has Hebrew school classes in four locations to meet the needs of families in different neighborhoods. While traditional membership is available at Tamid, the synagogue also offers a fee-for-service opportunity they call Neighbors and Friends, which is focused on religious school education, *b'nai mitzvah* tutoring and preparation, and High Holy Day service attendance. Here is how Tamid frames it: "We know that not everyone wants to be a synagogue member but we still want you to consider Tamid your Jewish home. That's why we've created the Neighbors and Friends program which welcomes you to participate-as-you-go."[2]

Temple Shalom

Woodbury, New York ▣ Reform ▣ Small

Temple Shalom was founded in 2011. Led by Rabbi Alan Stein, the congregation has been growing steadily in Suffolk County, New York (Long Island), where the overall Jewish population is otherwise in decline. Temple Shalom first held High Holy Day services in a local country club, outgrew the facility, and started meeting at the Suffolk YM/YWHA, mostly utilizing a fee-for-service model. The

---

How Is Temple Shalom Unique?

Temple Shalom is a warm inviting congregation with a father and son Rabbi/Cantor team. The services are uplifting and the families are welcoming! Temple Shalom is designed to be innovative to encourage many who are not affiliated with a synagogue due to exorbitant dues, building funds and other fees to become part of a unique congregation with modest dues and more of a "pay as you go" format. Rather than paying $2,500.00 per family for just dues plus a building fund (where all the services you don't need are included), initial family dues for Temple Shalom start at $360.00. Each person or family pays for the services they need and pays a modest fee for High Holy Day tickets. If you need a Baby-Naming, Bar/Bat Mitzvah, Wedding, Unveiling or Funeral, we will be happy to provide the service for you for a reasonable fee.

"How Is Temple Shalom Unique?" Temple Shalom website, http://templeshalomny.org/.

---

annual membership fee, $360, is far less than the national average. High Holy Day tickets may be purchased individually. Bar/bat mitzvah lessons cost $1,000, and Hebrew school costs $925 a year.

Highlights

The transactional model reflects the relationships many members participate in throughout their lives outside the synagogue. Thus, people are very familiar with this approach to everyday living. The transactional model forces the congregation to establish a financial value for all of the services they provide to members and potential members. It also requires people to pay only for the services that they use. This approach helps the congregation to realize "you get what you pay for." Leaders may think that this model would lead synagogue participants to feel "nickel-and-dimed," since they would be charged for almost everything. In reality, however, this model may actually minimize that sentiment. All services provided by the synagogue are covered by specific fees. Members pay only for the services they need and use.

1. The synagogue maintains a schedule of such fees and shares it publicly. There are no hidden costs.
2. The membership roster includes all those who have paid a fee for any service provided by the synagogue.

Frequently Asked Questions

Admittedly, some people will oppose the transactional model because it represents a radical break from the traditional membership-and-dues model. They may also be reluctant to adopt this model—or even explore it—because it reflects the growing fee-for-service norm in North America. Wise leaders will identify for these challengers the transactional relationships that are already in place in the synagogue—and in the Jewish community—and demonstrate that this model is simply a natural extension of what is already taking place. This model also helps members understand exactly what they are paying for by making explicit the material value of transactions. It may also make fundraising easier when everything has a clear expense; donors can plainly see what it costs to sponsor a certain number of lower-income families' involvement in various programs. Nevertheless, some people from the synagogue might think this model is "nickel-and-diming" in disguise. Considering this possibility, synagogue leaders may want to initially limit the scope of the various fees-for-service and then over time develop a more extensive list.

How do you determine whether a fee should be charged for a particular service provided by the synagogue?

In a transactional model, all services should be fee-based. Congregations might determine, however, that they want to make certain services available to everyone for free as a way of introducing the synagogue to potential participants.

How do you make the transition from a traditional membership model to the transactional model?

Synagogue leaders do not need to change everything at once. Once the specific services that will be fee-based have been selected and announced to the congregation and the community, segments of the community who might be the best target populations for those services (*b'nai mitzvah*, for example) can be identified and the change introduced to them. Then another service and membership segment would be chosen and the same process followed.

How do you advertise the services of your synagogue and maintain the dignity of the congregation?

While advertising the services of the synagogue may be easy, doing so while maintaining the dignity of the congregation may appear to be more challenging. A clear and concise message is recommended: "We respect your time and intelligence, so here's what our services cost, unobscured by layers of dues and fees. It's an easier entrance, but those who come will see that this is also the most sacred and meaningful community they've ever experienced...." Nevertheless, some synagogues may want to begin cautiously and advertise in less controversial venues before entering the mainstream. Just as other professionals advertise their services, synagogues can choose to invest in a media campaign and utilize the social media resources available to them. Synagogues can also determine where segments of the target population regularly spend their leisure time and recruit specifically in those places.

Implementation Steps

Step 1. Catalog the services and programs offered by the synagogue.

Step 2. Determine fees for each service or program based on current participation. Leaders might assign higher fees for high-volume participation to generate revenue based on current engagement trends, and assign lower fees to low-volume participation to encourage broader participation.

Step 3. Communicate synagogue services and fees to a wider community in the form of an à la carte menu.

Step 4. Review the participation of current members in the various programs offered by the synagogue. You may choose to segment the community and move one segment at a time into the fee-for-service model. Of course, that would mean that the selected segment might be assessed a sudden expense while the rest of the congregation goes on with "business as usual," but their cost for dues would be eliminated.

Step 5. Determine who takes advantage of a service (families with children in the preschool, for example) and market a complementary service (young-family programming) to them to get more people involved in more services that the synagogue offers.

Step 6. Analyze the transition. Measure service and program participation by the number of participants and frequency of participation. Track financial growth. Make changes in the cost of services if necessary.

Notes for Adapting This Model for Our Synagogue

In the building of the Tabernacle, all Israel were joined in their hearts; no one felt superior to the other.

Rabbi Mordecai Yosef Leiner of Izbica[1]
in a comment on Exodus 36:13

Why do synagogues matter? Simply put, they provide a place to meet three intrinsic human needs: the need to belong; the need to believe; and the need to become.... There should be in the synagogue a home for every Jew, irrespective of color, sex, status as an interfaith family, age or sexual orientation. Such a radically inclusive approach to community not only strengthens our community. It models Judaism's most central and enduring values of justice and compassion.

Rabbi David Cohen[2]

5

Open Membership

Why do people live close to a synagogue? For some, the choice is about their Sabbath observance. Others desire to live among other Jews, in a Jewish neighborhood or community. Yet for many others, the distance between their home and the local synagogue may be coincidental, based on a combination of factors, including available, affordable housing and proximity to facilities that meet their various needs and interests, such as the quality of local schools and workplaces. Aside from the specific reasons, in many communities, Jews live in the vicinity of a synagogue. We are not talking about the "old Jewish neighborhood," the kind that provided Jewish communal institutions within walking distance from home. But we are talking about a synagogue with a specific geographic sweep, what service providers refer to as a catchment area. When considering engagement and membership, these people and their families should be considered a target population or "low-hanging fruit," as some people like to call them. When the target population is defined by geography, leaders can more easily quantify their goals for synagogue engagement, because they have some idea of how many people they might reach.

An open membership model offers the benefit of membership to anyone in the community and thereby opens the doors to all. Combined with a program of outreach, it provides the congregation with the opportunity to engage large numbers of community residents. But this model requires a philosophical change in the institution. Because the target population is assumed to be part of the membership, the synagogue will need to focus on engaging those members rather than seeking new members.

Synagogues can provide open and free membership to all those who are Jewish or members of Jewish families who reside in a specified geographic area, which can be as large as synagogue leaders choose. All of these people can be counted on their membership rolls unless the individuals voice their disinterest and opt out. The open membership model lowers the cost barrier to the target population and prompts efforts to focus solely on geographic communities. By freely including everyone in the synagogue membership, as with the voluntary dues model, compulsory dues (and their relevance) cease to exist.

There is a common misconception that people do not value what they get for free. We believe that people do not value what is free *and* is perceived to have little or no value. That is not the case in all circumstances. People hold in high esteem things and experiences they think have great value even if they are also free, such as local parks and recreational areas or plays and concerts in public spaces. If people do not value what they pay for, that they paid in the first place is inconsequential.

If every member of a Jewish family in a specific area is considered to be a member of the synagogue, then two levels of membership might be established: the general, open, and free membership and a premium service membership for those who desire more out of the synagogue. Those who pay a premium for access provide revenue that underwrites the free participation of the general community. This open or free geographic membership model is often referred to as the freemium model. An alternative approach to this open membership model is that everyone receives the same basic services and everyone is charged set fees for additional services.

Leaders must first determine the geographic area to be served by the synagogue. In some settings, the boundaries may be quite apparent. In areas where there are multiple synagogues or blurry geographic boundaries, defining the service area might be more difficult. After you have determined the geographic parameters for your institution, you can provide open membership to all those who reside in the area. Current members will be automatically "grandfathered in," regardless of their place of residence.

Once the entire catalog of offerings from the synagogue has been identified, leaders of the synagogue can determine which services will be available to everyone in the community and which special programs and services will be included in an upgraded membership or offered on a fee-for-service basis. Standard and premium services or fees need to be identified before transitioning to an open membership model, regardless of the current model in place in the synagogue.

Note that if residents of an entire community are considered members of the synagogue, then fundraising—beyond the freemium model—can be conducted across the entire community and not limited to a smaller member pool as in the traditional membership model. Of course, this approach will likely not be welcomed by neighboring (and often competing) Jewish agencies and organizations. Thus it will be important to reach out to neighboring institutions to get them on board. As we like to say, however hackneyed the phrase may be, "a rising tide raises all ships." In other words, strong Jewish communal institutions make for a strong and vibrant Jewish community. As a result, everyone in the community can benefit.

Learning from the Tech World

The open membership model gains its inspiration from several sources, particularly the practice in the 1980s of sharing computer programs called freeware or shareware. Already in 1982, Andrew Fluegelman, associate editor of *PC Magazine,* described freeware as an "experiment in economics more than altruism."[3] But why would a software company give a product away? Users have the opportunity to try out the software before they make a long-term commitment (i.e., purchase) and are licensed to use the full version of the software. (Of course, some freeware is available without any payment required.) Nevertheless, those who purchase the product (or a license to use the product) subsidize the free software distributed to all those who are evaluating (and even potentially not purchasing) the product. In the synagogue, a smaller cohort of members contributes to the "greater good" of the community by underwriting the larger cohort's participation in the synagogue. This also makes good economic sense.

We can learn a lot from Skype's application of the freemium model. First released in August 2003 (in cooperation with those who developed Kazaa, an early peer-to-peer file sharing application following in the footsteps of Napster, the pioneer in music file sharing), Skype attempted to revolutionize the peer-to-peer environment (Sky Peer-to-Peer, Skype's originally proposed name) by enabling users to make free video calls. Although Skype has expanded today to offer file-transfer and videoconferencing services, the freemium concept was the basis for Skype's two-tier model: free in-network voice calls and premium out-of-network calling, with the revenue from premium users underwriting the free service for basic users. Skype customers can speak for free to anyone who also uses Skype; however, if customers want to use Skype to call someone who does not have Skype, customers will be charged for that service. Similarly, people can use Skype for a video chat between individuals using two computers. However, if people want to use Skype for a videoconference call involving more than two locations, then all users of the videoconference call must pay for an upgrade to their service. The conference calls cover the costs of the computer-to-computer calls. As a result of this freemium approach, Skype has disrupted international telecommunications businesses, especially those that sell "instant messaging," which was widely promoted by Internet pioneer America Online (AOL).

For some synagogue leaders, the changes suggested in this chapter may be motivated by economics more than altruism. Nevertheless, the approach suggested in this chapter will be beneficial to the welfare of the community. Reframing the relationship between a synagogue and its members is vital to the future survival and success of a congregation. We made mention of this notion earlier in this book, particularly in reference to Dr. Ron Wolfson's important book *Relational Judaism*. Nonetheless, it warrants emphasis here, since any change in membership structures will require further enhancement of the relationship between members and the synagogue. People don't relate to institutions. People relate to one another. Yet these individuals do indeed represent the entirety of the institution in their reaction to the other, especially to the newcomer.

The Community Library and Swimming Pool

While no Jewish communal institutions of which we are aware have established the open membership model, although we have been speaking about it for many years—and Allan Finkelstein of the JCC Association has, with us, translated our message for the JCCs—we should recognize that the model works quite well for some secular community institutions. The Jewish community could take its lead from these organizations. For example, anyone who lives in a community, usually defined by municipal boundaries, can use the local library. Those who live outside the municipality are sometimes given the opportunity pay a fee to join the library, and some libraries offer premium memberships for a higher fee. Premium memberships include longer library loan privileges, for example, or the opportunity to borrow a larger number of books. These fees help pay for the cost of the free open memberships for the others.

Some community swimming pools operate in a similar way. Residents of the local community are given free access to the swimming pool, while others have to pay for access. However, should the resident want a premium service, such as swimming lessons, towel service, a locker, or access to the adjacent tennis courts, an annual membership fee might be required, although some communities charge individual fees for such services.

Highlights

1. Open membership automatically identifies as members everyone in a specific geographic area.
2. Synagogues will need to clarify which services are basic—available to all members—and which are select services available only to those who have opted for a premium upgrade. It is because of the possibility of a premium upgrade that the model is sometimes called a freemium model.
3. Those who opt for premium services provide the financial foundation of the synagogue for the remainder of the members.

Frequently Asked Questions

As alluded to in the questions below, the chief stumbling block to the successful implementation of the open membership model may be the objections of neighboring Jewish institutions, including the Jewish Federation, the Jewish Community Center, and of course other synagogues. Many, if not all, of these Jewish communal institutions will likely feel threatened by one synagogue's adoption of this model. While the open membership model is not explicitly an outreach strategy, other institutions may see it as a move by the synagogue adopting the model to aggressively recruit new members. To avoid any antagonism, synagogue leaders may want to coordinate their efforts with local institutions. When sharing the model with these institutions, leaders should assure their neighbors that the adoption of the model is not an attempt to cannibalize their membership. Since the majority of those in the Jewish community are not affiliated with synagogues, there are many people to engage without having a negative impact on any other local institution.

What if there's more than one synagogue in a geographic catchment area?

No two synagogues are the same, and synagogues already compete with one another and engage in "turf battles." If there is more than one synagogue in a geographic area, then more than one synagogue may embrace this model. If several in an area adopt this model, then each synagogue will have to clarify and communicate its unique mission.

What if people don't live in the catchment area and still want to participate in the synagogue that offers open membership?

Those who don't live in the geographic catchment area of the synagogue are not part of its target population. The synagogue should not deviate from its goals and objectives specifically to serve individuals who do not live in these areas. However, the synagogue should be open to the participation and membership of those who live outside the catchment area, regardless of whether there are other synagogues in the area where they live. Synagogue leaders may want to include membership for those outside the catchment area as part of freemium services.

Can you be given open membership if you are not Jewish?

Those who come from other religious backgrounds and are married to Jews or live in a Jewish family household may participate in the open membership model. Although an independent individual from another faith background who lives in the catchment area is not part of the target audience for this membership model, this individual may ask to participate and perhaps be a member. Those who are on a religious journey toward Judaism, perhaps already participating in the synagogue and interested in conversion, would be considered part of the target population.

Implementation Steps

Step 1. Outline your catchment area on a map. Identify the greatest needs and desires in your catchment area. Refocus your synagogue's programming to reach solely that defined community.

Step 2. Determine which basic services your synagogue offers that are most appealing. Define the free basic membership using a combination of these two analyses. The basic membership should include programs that address one of the greatest needs and desires in the area in order to attract people to the synagogue, leaving the other needs and desires to be addressed by premium membership.

Step 3. Determine which services your synagogue offers already that are considered premium (or perhaps should be). Then develop services and programs to be made available for the premium level.

Step 4. Determine how many basic members have to become premium members in order to raise the funds necessary to operate and maintain the synagogue. Synagogue leaders set that number of premium members as a recruitment goal.

Step 5. Develop marketing materials that reflect the new membership model. Then market the new model to the general community.

Notes for Adapting This Model for Our Synagogue

The synagogue ... helps us in our quest for God, to evoke our sense of the sacred, to enhance our capacity to respond with wonderment to the essential mystery of life.

attributed to Rabbi Alexander Schindler[1]

A civilization cannot be handed down in privacy. It cannot be handed down just by reading books. To thrive, culture must be lived.... The setting for many important facets of Jewish civilization—eating, child-rearing, and Shabbat observance, for example—is the family. But the family cannot learn and sustain even these aspects of Jewish living by itself, and much of Judaism cannot be experienced just within the family. The only plausible setting for much of Jewish living is the community.

Rabbi David A. Teutsch[2]

6

The No-Membership Model

In a no-membership model for synagogues, anyone can participate in the programs the synagogue offers and take advantage of the services provided without paying dues. A corps of regular synagogue participants will undoubtedly emerge, but they will not be called members. They are participants like everyone else—even if they become active participants. This synagogue model allows synagogue leaders to focus on deepening the engagement of all interested and active participants, rather than concentrating on attracting individuals to affiliate with the institution as dues-paying members. Such engagement should focus, for example, on people's relationship to the sacred and their service to their neighbors. Any potential dichotomy between members and nonmembers is eliminated in the no-membership model. Of course, funds will still have to be raised to support the institution.

Synagogue leaders often say that many programs are open to anyone and that one doesn't have to be a member to participate. That's true for many offerings, such as daily and Shabbat worship services. However, were someone to attend those services regularly, a congregational representative would probably solicit the frequent attendee for membership, since synagogue leaders are concerned about the financial security of the institution and believe there is intrinsic value in synagogue membership. Open programs are usually those that, in fact, are not engaging the majority of members, so leaders feel comfortable opening them up to nonmembers. But the model we are describing is markedly different. It involves no membership at all.

For the majority of institutions in the community—whether within or outside the Jewish community, for-profit or not-for-profit—this approach may not sound unusual. Consider organizations that exist primarily to serve people and are not interested in making a profit. They have no membership, only participants whose goal is to fulfill the prescribed mission of the organization.

Chabad

The most well-known example of the no-membership model in the Jewish community is Chabad. Most Chabad centers have no membership. Programs and services are open to anyone. Chabad centers survive financially through what may be described as relationship fundraising, or better, "friendraising" that leads to fundraising. Chabad's rabbis are social entrepreneurs who succeed or fail based on their appeal in the marketplace, generally independent of boards of directors. The rabbis determine their budget and what funds are needed, and then they seek out and solicit only those who have the capacity to make a meaningful gift to the institution. They do not depend on members to fund their work. Most Chabad programs are free, although there may be a minimal charge for some programs, with everyone paying the same amount. In a few locations, such as in Boynton Beach, Florida, Chabad has attempted to mimic the prevailing American synagogue model, but most of these experiments in traditional synagogue membership models have ended in financial failure. It seems that people have not been accustomed to supporting Chabad through the traditional membership-and-dues model. And Chabad is not interested in building a traditional membership model. Rather, their explicit mission is to recruit active participants in their programs and services without regard to membership.

Manhattan Jewish Experience

New York City ▣ Orthodox ▣ Medium

A prime example of a no-membership synagogue is Manhattan Jewish Experience (MJE), founded by Rabbi Mark N. Wildes in 1998. MJE is housed in The Jewish Center (an Orthodox synagogue, not to be confused with the Jewish Community Center in Manhattan).

MJE's programs include those focused on Jews who live on the East Side and Downtown in New York City. According to their own publicity, MJE is a program primarily for those in their twenties and thirties "with little or no background in Judaism interested in connecting more to each other, to Judaism and to the community at large."[3] Since they opened, MJE has served over 14,000 participants.

Nashuva

Los Angeles, California ▣ Independent ▣ Large

Rather than being called a synagogue, Nashuva is an independent prayer community, according to founder Rabbi Naomi Levy. Founded in Los Angeles in 2004, this community comprises 1,000 people. There are no dues and no membership. As a result, no voting rights are afforded to participants. All of their services and programs are open to anyone who wants to participate. Nashuva meets once a month on Friday evening to welcome Shabbat, as well as monthly for a social action project. They also provide prayer services for the holidays, and there are no tickets for the High Holy Days. During a recent service for the High Holy Days that was also streamed online, 500 people attended, but 200,000 people viewed the service online.[4]

Participation at Nashuva

If I go, will I be asked for money? For membership? Are there any dues?

Nashuva is supported entirely by contributions, but people can give (or not) of their own free will. Please understand that Nashuva is a very different kind of community: there are no dues, no membership, no tickets. Everyone is welcome and we offer our monthly Shabbat services to the entire community, so everyone can enjoy the wisdom and beauty of Judaism. But, to do so, we rely on—we need—your support and encourage donations.

"Frequently Asked Questions," Nashuva website, www.nashuva.com/nashuvafaq.html#9.

Pop-Ups

One version of the no-membership model is the so-called pop-up, which is generally established for specific purposes, such as High Holy Day services, Passover seders, or Hanukkah celebrations. Pop-ups can also be found in summer and holiday resort locations. In the commercial environment, pop-ups often appear just before civil and religious holidays such as Fourth of July (firework stands), Halloween (pumpkin patches and corn mazes), and Christmas (Christmas tree lots). In Israel, these short-term businesses "pop up" before Hanukkah and Purim. Restaurants may offer pop-ups in heavily trafficked areas, so potential customers can sample their menu offerings. The original motivation behind retail pop-ups was twofold: retailers, especially big-box stores, needed to find ways to get into local markets without making significant investments, and businesses could take advantage of short-term leases landlords offered for vacant spaces.

One example of a pop-up synagogue is Ohel Ayalah in the New York City area. Founded by Rabbi Judith Hauptman, a professor at The Jewish Theological Seminary, Ohel Ayalah (named to honor Hauptman's mother's memory) was established to offer a free walk-in service to meet the needs of those in their twenties and thirties who do not have a place to pray on the High Holy Days. As the rabbinic leader of Ohel Ayalah, Hauptman understands that it is possible to wake up on Rosh Hashanah morning and say, "I feel like going to the synagogue today," having made no previous arrangements. Ohel Ayalah offers such free worship services at pop-up locations in Brooklyn, Manhattan, and Queens. As a result of the positive response of participants, Ohel Ayalah started offering Passover seders (at full and discounted prices) and Hanukkah and Purim (first drink free) parties as well. The majority of the program is supported by foundation grants and individual donors.

The Mega-Donor Model

Another variation on the no-membership model is what we call the mega-donor model, in which the institution is supported by one or more substantial donors. Sixth & I in Washington, DC (built in 1908, rededicated in 2004), uses the mega-donor model. Originally the home of Adas Israel Congregation, now located elsewhere in Washington, the building at Sixth and I was owned and occupied for a time by Turner Memorial AME Church. When the church put it up for sale, three local businessmen—Douglas Jemal, Abe Pollin, and Shelton Zuckerman—decided that it should not be sold, for fear it would be destroyed or used as a nightclub (the desire of one of its possible purchasers) as the neighborhood gentrified.

The restored synagogue underwent several programmatic iterations and changes in administrative leadership as they targeted different populations. Their program initially included worship services led by guest rabbis. Now with their own rabbinic and program staff, Sixth & I is solely focused on people in their twenties and thirties and is not planning on aging in place along with their program participants. Instead, they will hand off their participants to local institutions and work with the neighboring synagogues to make changes in their programs and services that respond to the needs and desires of the twenties to thirties population—even as they age. While Sixth & I has no membership and many of their programs may best be described as fee-for-service, the synagogue's model would not be considered transactional (as described in chapter 4), since 60 percent of the support (in 2014, according to the executive director,

---

Participation at Sixth & I

Can I become a member of Sixth & I?

As an innovative organization seeking to reimagine the Jewish experience, Sixth & I is a nonmembership synagogue without a congregational structure. Anyone is welcome to join our ever-growing community by participating in our à la carte programs.

"Frequently Asked Questions," Sixth & I website, www.sixthandi.org/about/frequently-asked-questions/.

Esther Safran Foer) still comes from major donors and grants. To gain further financial supporters among participants, the synagogue introduced a new program called Team 6: "Designed for young professionals, Team 6 is a chance to be a supporter, an influencer, and a connector. Joining Team 6 will help extend Sixth & I's reach to a growing community interested in all things spiritual and cultural."[5] Team 6 includes six giving levels, from the Fan level at $180 ($15/month) through the VIP level at $2,400 ($200/month). Each level has its own benefits, such as priority ticketing for High Holy Day services for the All-Star level $600 ($50/month).

Highlights

The no-membership model allows anyone in a community to participate in anything that the synagogue has to offer without paying for membership. Thus, it lowers or even removes the barrier of cost to participate. Although some may see the lack of membership as a negative aspect of the model, a counterbalancing positive is that synagogue leaders do not need to spend time on membership recruitment, thus affording them the opportunity to focus on developing programs and services that will meet the needs of their constituents.

1. The no-membership synagogue model—as can be discerned by its name—has no members. Thus, the synagogue's focus is not on the recruitment of members, but on the engagement of participants.
2. Because the synagogue has no members, people are not expected to pay dues. Thus, the energy that is expended on dues collection can be redirected to raising funds from a broader population. However, no-member synagogues can charge for services as needed, keeping in mind that charging fees can raise a barrier for some potential participants.
3. No-membership institutions can more easily serve various specific target populations, such as those in their twenties and thirties.

Frequently Asked Questions

The greatest resistance to the no-membership model will probably come from those active and longtime members of the synagogue who believe membership in a synagogue is a value unto itself because it brings Jews in contact with one another and helps create community. They also believe that people affirm their Jewish identity through synagogue membership. Leaders need to help those who are already invested in the synagogue understand that the move to the no-membership model will help sustain and grow the synagogue by broadening the base of potential supporters and engaging them. This expansion is particularly important at a time when the synagogue's continued viability is being threatened, especially in the context of a growing North American culture in which people are avoiding membership in many institutions—religious, cultural, or otherwise. Other resisters will fear that it will be hard to develop a synagogue community without members since participants will not be able to develop a relationship with the institution. Leaders will need to assure detractors that a sense of belonging is determined by whether people feel welcomed, at home and among friends, and engaged by a community of meaning.

How does a no-member institution keep track of participants and follow them on their journey through life?

Leaders are encouraged to implement database systems that allow staff members and volunteers to follow participants on their Jewish journey. If a synagogue puts energy into building relationships, keeping track of folks will be easier.

How do leaders and staff in synagogues using the no-membership model build relationships among people if they are not members?

Relationship building is much easier to do in smaller institutions, especially if participants become regulars. However, as is suggested by the motto of the organization

New York Cares, "Getting smaller as we grow," large no-member synagogues will have to form smaller affinity groups to bring people closer to one another. This issue is related to the size of the synagogue rather than the particular membership model.

Implementation Steps

Step 1. Create a financial resource development plan to replace the income from dues.

Step 2. Target the largest population segment that contributes the least amount of income to the synagogue. Change their membership status first, but secure their participation in an affinity group. Then follow with other segments of your membership.

Step 3. Analyze the new model. Measure participant involvement—number of participants and frequency of participation.

Notes for Adapting This Model for Our Synagogue

The future of the Jewish community depends on Jews to step across the threshold, not to trip or falter, and to find their place in the synagogue. We will all be enriched by their participation and involvement.

Alan Teperow[1]

Synagogue membership is a responsibility shared by both the synagogue staff and its members. The responsibility of the synagogue is to provide meaningful, engaging, spiritually invigorating prayer services, learning opportunities and other gatherings of significance. But it is also incumbent on members to avail themselves of these opportunities and to engage the synagogue as a place where they connect as Jews and become inspired by the gifts of active participation.

Rabbi Adam J. Raskin[2]

7

The Tiered Model

The tiered model is a developmental or expanding model of membership. In this model, synagogue membership is available for a basic fee, and additional services, arranged in tiers, are available for higher fees. As members use more services (for which they pay), they become more involved in the institution. But everyone is welcome to participate in worship. The primary benefit of this model is that it allows leaders to assume a base level of income and to attend to clusters of programs, rather than having to focus on individual programs as in a fee-for-service model. This may seem like more of an advantage to synagogue leaders than synagogue members, but it does provide members with an alternative approach to their membership than is afforded by the other models presented in this book.

Consider this example. Each member is charged a $1,000 basic membership fee and receives regular communication from the synagogue and access to Shabbat services, holiday/festival services, and celebrations. The next tier of membership, for which a member pays an additional $1,000 ($2,000 total), includes lifecycle events, such as weddings, funerals, baby namings, and so forth. If the member wants access to educational opportunities, such as *b'nai mitzvah* training, religious school, preschool, and the like, the total membership fee is $3,000. Other membership services can be added as well, in more tiers.

While this may look like a fee-for-service model, the models are quite different. With the tiered model, synagogue leaders, recognizing that similar population segments often opt for the same group of services, can create different levels of membership based on clusters of services designed for that segment's needs. It allows those on the periphery of the institution to pay for groups of services, rather than individual ones. Furthermore, this model helps the institution determine budget priorities based on the number of people who are interested in particular clusters of services. For example, if few members join particular tiers, staff might not spend energy and synagogue resources in the areas included in those tiers, such as enhancing holiday celebrations for boomers. They can instead focus on potential members' and members' desire for a strong preschool program and other associated programs that would be attractive to this population segment.

While comparing a synagogue to a car wash might seem odd, the various packages of services offered at car washes provide a useful parallel to tiered membership. The different tiers provide customers with different levels of service. Some car washes even offer what could be thought of as a membership model that allows unlimited access to specific services for a monthly or yearly fee.

Temple Beth Hillel–Beth El

Wynnewood, Pennsylvania ▣ Conservative ▣ Medium

Temple Beth Hillel–Beth El offers members two different sets of tier options. The first set of tiers is the Traditional Commitment option. As the synagogue website explains, it is "a membership fee based on a member's age and marital status. A single member pays at a lower rate than a married member, and discounts apply for members who are over age 65, as well as for our members under 35."[3] In the second set of tiers, called a Patron Commitment option, the names of the tiers reflect the relationship of the member to the congregation: Benefactor, Sustainer, Builder, and Guardian. Benefits are added to each successively higher tier. While High Holy Day tickets are included in both sets of tiers, tickets to educational programs and synagogue dinners, guest tickets for the High Holy Days, and reserved parking spaces are offered to only specific member categories within each tier. Moreover, the congregation has made a promise to those in the Patron

Temple Beth Hillel–Beth El Community Circle Commitment Model

This model was created in response to requests from many of our members to simplify their support of the important work of the synagogue. It allows the professional staff and volunteers to spend more time developing quality programs, fostering warm relationships, providing needed services and creating meaningful opportunities for spiritual growth, and less time raising money. It allows us to operate with greater predictability regarding revenue for the coming year. Moreover, a Patron Commitment recognizes that TBH-BE is a deserving recipient of your philanthropy.

We know that our Patron Commitment options will not work for every member. Therefore, our Traditional Commitment options retain all of the features of our historical model of dues plus fundraising.

Our Community Circle Commitment Model is designed so that all members can find a comfortable way to support our congregation. It is our hope that the circle will grow and embrace all who choose to be a part of Temple Beth Hillel–Beth El.

"Temple Beth Hillel–Beth El Community Circle Commitment Model," www.tbhbe.org/wp-content/uploads/2013/09/TBHBEcommitcircle13.pdf.

Commitment tiers that they will not receive additional solicitations for funds. In late 2014, synagogue leaders established a cooperative relationship with the local Jewish Community Center, entitling all members of the synagogue to a free three-month membership at the JCC.

The Vilna Shul

Boston, Massachusetts ▣ Independent ▣ Small

The Vilna Shul in Boston is a synagogue—although it is also called a "center for Jewish culture"—that offers seven membership tiers. The Vilna Shul was established by Eastern European

Jewish immigrants who came to Boston in 1893, settling in the Beacon Hill neighborhood and forming a *landsmanschaft* (a fellowship group of immigrants from the same community). They gathered together for prayer services in one another's homes. As their numbers increased, they established a synagogue. After several moves, they built a building on Philips Street, where the synagogue is currently located. However, the neighborhood around it changed (the city razed the area in an urban renewal project), leaving the Vilna Shul as the only synagogue in the area. In the meantime, Jews left the area as well, and the last worship service, prior to a renaissance, was held at the Vilna Shul in 1985. When the synagogue reopened, it did so as a cultural center, housing various museum exhibits and hosting the Havurah on the Hill (HOH). The latter, founded in 2002, provides monthly Shabbat services as well as holiday celebrations and services for young Jewish adults. HOH requires no membership and does not charge dues. However, HOH does request donations for their monthly Shabbat dinners. The various tiers of membership for the cultural center include some of these Shabbat dinners. The more expensive membership tiers include more guest passes for Shabbat dinners as a benefit.

American Alliance of Museums

The American Alliance of Museums has four categories of members: individual, museum, ally, and industry. The membership option for museums, the Alliance's primary constituency group, is tiered. The Alliance develops standards for museums and best practices for museum program staff. It provides resources to museums and career development guidance for staff members. It also functions as an advocate for museums. The Alliance explains, "Your level of engagement increases with each tier, as do the benefits and rewards—for your museum, your staff and you."[4] Services are organized as follows: Tier 1—the basics, including access to information about ethics, standards, and best practices for personnel; Tier 2—enhanced access, including ideas for museum innovation and professional development; Tier 3—the full suite of benefits, including all that the Alliance has to offer.

Highlights

The tiered membership model allows individuals and families to increase their financial commitment to the synagogue as their relationship with the synagogue deepens and intensifies. This model reflects the various stations in the lives of individuals and families, but it does not require the synagogue to make assumptions about their membership needs and how much they want to financially support the synagogue based on either age or socioeconomic status.

1. All potential members join the synagogue as members and pay a basic membership fee in the tiered model.
2. For additional services and opportunities for engagement, people join at higher membership levels or tiers.
3. Tiered levels help shape the programmatic areas of focus for a congregation.

Frequently Asked Questions

To avoid minimizing the value of the membership in the tiered model, people need to understand that "basic membership" is a foundational membership in the synagogue. Some people will look at synagogue membership as an all-or-nothing proposition and think that members have an obligation to support the entire synagogue institution, whether or not they make use of all of the available services. The tiered model offers a gradual path toward full engagement, as well as capturing those who might be inclined to withdraw their membership when their own needs change. This approach is particularly valuable to those at the ends of the family-life continuum—those starting families on the one end and those who become "empty nesters" on the other—as well as those who seek out only single membership.

What if a person wants the services offered in a higher level and not a lower level?

The tiered model presents graduated membership services based on a developmental approach. The tiers should be constructed in such a way that after participants take advantage of the services offered at level 1, they will be ready to take on the services provided in level 2. The content and pricing of each level should reflect the needs and resources of the target population. However, the middle tiers—for those who usually have the most needs (education, life-cycle events, and the like) but often the least discretionary income—need to be designed and priced especially carefully.

How is the cost of each tier determined?

Determine the synagogue's cost for each service, and divide it by the number of people who use it, as if you were determining a fee for that service. Then add up the fees for all services to be included in a tier to get the total cost of that tier.

What is the risk in implementing this model?

The most challenging aspect in implementing this model is projecting the number of potential members per tier.

Implementation Steps

Step 1. Determine the cost of your base tier. You can do this by taking your operating expenses and dividing it by the total number of member households.

Step 2. Identify the various population segments of your membership. Break them down by age, life station, and interest.

Step 3. Design a tier for each population segment that takes into account the ways people in that segment most frequently engage with the synagogue. As appropriate, combine segments to limit the number of tiers and keep the system simple for members.

Step 4. Estimate the number of tier cohorts and project their size—the number of households (or individuals) you think will be involved in each cohort.

Step 5. Develop marketing materials that reflect the new membership model, and implement a marketing plan.

Notes for Adapting This Model for Our Synagogue

The [purpose of the] synagogue is to open up your eyes to the world.

Rabbi Harold Schulweis[1]

We must step into the shoes of someone who only comes to synagogue once a year and feels out of place, like a tourist who doesn't understand the language of the local population.

Rabbi Ronen Neuwirth[2]

8

Special-Interest Membership

Anyone who has been involved in synagogue life, especially in a leadership role, understands that not every aspect of synagogue life will be relevant or of interest to everyone. In fact, synagogues are classically referred to in three ways—as *beit knesset* (meeting place, which musician Craig Taubman creatively translates as "entry point"), *beit tefillah* (prayer house), and *beit midrash* (house of study or academy of learning)—suggesting that the synagogue functions for different people in different ways. As a result, potential members of the synagogue may be interested in only select aspects of the institution. The special-interest model allows people to become members in only those areas of the synagogue that interest and engage them. However, the goal is to engage potential members rather than simply solicit them for membership.

The special-interest membership model is also referred to as the bundled model. The special-interest model allows members to join for select purposes, such as the High Holy Days or perhaps bar/bat mitzvah only, that can be "bundled" together. While expanding its base, the synagogue can also use these bundles to learn which areas of synagogue life are attractive to potential members. A synagogue may want to expand or enrich highly valued programs and services and discontinue those that do not attract potential members. To be sure, synagogues may nonetheless offer programs with low participation if leaders believe those programs are integral to the foundation of synagogue or Jewish life. Memberships could be priced so that special interests with greater participation subsidize the cost of maintaining special-interest groups with lower involvement.

The special-interest model permits members to group together various aspects of the institutional program to form a customized membership. By allowing for the bundling of special interests, members wouldn't have to discontinue their relationship with a synagogue when certain aspects of membership no longer appeal to them or are needed by them. Rather, members can simply subscribe to different bundles as their interests evolve. Members with similar bundles would form natural spheres of engagement (social groups or *chavurot*). These organic social groups would create smaller subcommunities within the larger synagogue community. All members of all special interests would be given the right to vote on all synagogue matters.

Temple Emanu-El of South Beach

Miami Beach, Florida ▣ Conservative ▣ Small

Although the membership model of Temple Emanu-El of South Beach is fairly traditional—with giving levels spread over age groups—the Hebrew school is available to nonmembers. Philosophically, the synagogue sees the religious education of children as an outreach opportunity, recognizing that families are often introduced to synagogue life through Hebrew school. Therefore, for a tuition fee of $300, nonmember families are permitted to participate in the Hebrew school and attend High Holy Day services. In effect, Temple Emanu-El offers a bundled bar mitzvah training/High Holy Day membership package alongside the traditional synagogue membership model. (The synagogue, like other Sunbelt institutions, also offers a seasonal or "snowbird" membership for members who live in Florida only during the winter.)

Shir Hadash Synagogue

Wheeling, Illinois ▣ Reconstructionist ▣ Small

Shir Hadash Synagogue leaders made a decision in 2014 to discontinue selling High Holy Day tickets. Instead, Shir Hadash offers what we may think of as a special-interest membership just for the holidays. According to their website, the congregation is offering for $54 a High Holy Day membership that includes everything Shir Hadash has to offer between Selichot (penitential prayers prior to Rosh Hashanah) and Simchat Torah—that is, all worship services, including Rosh Hashanah and Yom Kippur, as well as the congregation's Lunch and Learn with the Rabbi on Thursdays and adult education on Sunday mornings for this period only.

Lab/Shul

New York City ▣ Independent ▣ Small

Established by Amichai Lau-Lavie, the founder of Storahtelling and now a rabbinical student at The Jewish Theological Seminary, Lab/Shul in New York City is described as "an everybody friendly, artist-driven, experimental community for sacred Jewish gatherings ... dedicated to exploring, creating and celebrating innovative opportunities for contemplation, life-cycle rituals, the arts, lifelong learning and social justice."[3] While categorizing Lab/Shul's membership-and-dues model is difficult, it can best be described as a special-interest membership. Those who purchase what Lab/Shul calls a "season pass" are entitled to seats at all High Holy Day worship events, as well as holiday events throughout the year. The pass also provides access to a monthly study salon series and four Shabbat ritual events, one each season, at a synagogue leader's home. Lab/Shul suggests contribution ranges, based on the makeup of families and their life station: individual, $750–$3,600; couple, $1,000–$4,000; family with one parent, $950–$3,800; and family with two parents, $1,400–$4,500. High Holy Day tickets can also be purchased separately. While Lab/Shul does not have a school, it does provide *b'nai mitzvah* training as part of its "Raising the Bar" program, for which there are additional charges.

Oak Ridge Country Club

Hopkins, Minnesota

Country clubs often use the special-interest model for membership. The mission statement of Oak Ridge Country Club, founded in

1921, includes an affirmation of Jewish values. The club offers three kinds of membership: full golf, sports activity, and dining. Members are able to choose one, two, or three special interests to customize their membership. Because many Jewish—and other—country clubs throughout the country price membership the way Oak Ridge does, many synagogue members are well acquainted with the special-interest membership model through that experience.

Institute of Electrical and Electronic Engineers (IEEE)

The IEEE (referred to as I-triple-E) is the world's largest technical professional association. As a result, it has a diverse membership composed of engineers, scientists, and allied professionals, including computer scientists, software developers, information technology professionals, physicists, medical doctors, and many more. To meet the varied needs and desires of its constituency, IEEE offers memberships in thirty-eight special-interest "societies," each with a specific technical or professional focus, such as IEEE Publications, IEEE Technical Councils, IEEE Technical Communities, and more. IEEE sees this approach as the way for its participants to "get the most out of their membership."[4]

Highlights

The special-interest membership model provides an incentive for people to remain members as their needs and the needs and interests of family members change. It is among the more flexible of synagogue membership models.

1. In this model, all members personalize their connection and involvement in the synagogue and pay for only the selected level of involvement.
2. The special-interest membership model provides the opportunity for potential members to shape their membership according to their needs and interests.

Frequently Asked Questions

Some people who do not support the special-interest membership model argue that exposing people to the multiplicity of offerings of the synagogue, even when they are interested in only one, will open them up to the possibility of taking advantage of more—and eventually all—that the synagogue has to offer. Leaders need to help these critics understand that the synagogue needs to be multifaceted so it can serve people's various needs. Leaders also need to educate those who object to the model that when the synagogue requires people who are interested in only one or two services to pay for a full membership, the synagogue risks not engaging that individual or family at all—and even losing that member. Finally, special-interest members may also change their interests over time, and the membership model is flexible enough to follow the individual and family over the course of their lives. This model allows for a longer-term, specialized membership that meets the specific needs of members.

Is this really a fee-for-service model?

It is similar to the fee-for-service model, but the fees are grouped according to the special interests of members. Bar and bat mitzvah membership may, for example, include the life-cycle event itself as well as all of the education and preparation leading up to the event.

Can someone be involved if they don't pay for that "interest"?

This model may unfortunately create an environment of elitist groups in the synagogue, contrary to the best practices of warm and welcoming engagement. This may make some congregations uncomfortable. But if the synagogue wants to create a special-interest model and some people are unwilling to pay, synagogue leaders may want to exclude them. However, if some members are unable to pay, then provisions should of course be made by the synagogue's board to accommodate their needs. The notion of exclusive access could also attract some potential members.

Can someone "rebundle" at any time?

The individual synagogue would have to determine whether to permit membership changes. Members should be able to add "interests" into their bundle at any time, but a synagogue might allow them to withdraw or remove interests only at the end of the synagogue's fiscal or membership year.

Can synagogues establish a minimum "interest" or fee? And is any part of the synagogue's services and programs "free"?

Again, the synagogue will have to reflect on their financial needs and make this decision. One might assume that attendance at Shabbat services or daily minyan is free. A synagogue may decide to include a certain category of "interests" by default in every bundle, or it might close its doors to nonmembers altogether.

Implementation Steps

Step 1. Determine which interests are significant enough that people would be willing to pay for membership that gives them access to those services and programs. Then discern which special interests are related to one another, and bundle them.

Step 2. Determine the cost for each special-interest membership.

Step 3. Establish a base cost for each special membership and bundle. All bundles could be priced the same, or they could be priced differently, depending on how much time is required of the clergy and staff and for use of the building for each special-interest group. You may want to take the total budget of the synagogue and divide it by the number of special interests.

Step 4. Develop marketing materials that reflect the new membership model.

Notes for Adapting This Model for Our Synagogue

Hillel said: Do not separate yourself from the community.

Pirke Avot 2:4

If we consider community as a "coming together," then we are one—a single entity comprised of many different and equally important parts. It means we welcome and celebrate our diversity, while realizing we are much more together than alone. Community is as much a celebration of how we differ as it is a celebration of what unifies us. It is a commitment to doing what is in our collective best interests, to determining what these interests are, and to making the impossible possible.

Kirk Wisemayer[1]

9

The Community Campus

An Approach to Financing Institutional Physical Structure

Many synagogues were built at a time when leaders felt the need for architecturally significant buildings with large sanctuaries and numerous religious school classrooms. This reflected their desire to make a statement that they, as Americans, were equal to other religious groups in their communities. As these needs have changed, some synagogues have sought to rent their space to institutions unrelated to the synagogue or its mission. Others have modified their buildings by adding more intimate chapel spaces to accommodate smaller groups, particularly those who gather for a Shabbat that is not enhanced by a bar/bat mitzvah, holiday celebration, or other festive occasion. This chapter is more about the structure of the synagogue institution than it is about membership. But because the maintenance of the physical structure of the synagogue is intimately tied to the financial needs of the congregation, which are the responsibility of its members, this chapter has implications for the conversation about membership and revenue.

In the Babylonian Talmud, the Rabbis taught, "A *talmid chakham* [Torah scholar] is not allowed to live in a city that does not have these ten things: a *beit din* [court of law] that metes out punishments; a *tzedekah* [charitable giving] fund that is collected by two people and distributed by three people; a synagogue; a bath house; a toilet; a physician; a craftsperson; a blood-letter; [some versions add:] a butcher; and a teacher of children" (Babylonian Talmud, *Sanhedrin* 17b). Thus, we should not be surprised that numerous communities include a Jewish community campus, usually with the Jewish Federation or Jewish Community Center as the anchor institution that serves as the landlord for the entire enterprise. In most cases some Federation-supported agencies also occupy spaces on the campus, but in only a few locations are synagogues included. These community campuses are established based on the intrinsic value of collaboration and the desire to practice fiscal responsibility by consolidating resources.

In the community campus model, which is particularly attractive to once-large institutions with big physical plants, the synagogue forms an independent corporation whose responsibility it is to maintain the campus. The congregation then becomes one of the tenants renting space on that campus. All tenants would adhere to a general mission stipulated by the corporation and would control only their private space. Shared space would be governed by the independent corporation. Leaders of the community campus would actively seek out like-minded institutions or organizations to provide services that might benefit all members.

This community campus might include buildings in addition to those already owned by synagogues or other institutions in the Jewish community. It might also relocate to a neutral space, so new tenants don't feel that they are moving onto a property already identified with another institution. Relocation may appeal to a synagogue whose membership has moved out of the neighborhood where the synagogue is or whose physical structure is in need of major refurbishing. Creating a new campus instead of using an existing structure may appeal to synagogues whose physical plants no longer serve the needs of its membership.

Some synagogues are renting out their facilities just to survive. For example, Temple Judea Mizpah (Reform) in Skokie, Illinois, was once a midsize synagogue of 500 families that has dwindled to under 200 families. They are now renting space to an Orthodox school. In addition, they have leased classrooms to serve as a satellite location for the early childhood program of the Arie Crown

Hebrew Day School. Similarly, Temple Israel in New Rochelle, New York, a Reform synagogue, rents space to an Orthodox day school called the Westchester Torah Academy. Rather than renting their school to another institution, however, Temple Emeth, a Reform synagogue in Teaneck, New Jersey, actually changed their program to accommodate a growing number of Orthodox students in their preschool and to attract the large Orthodox Jewish contingent in the community. Union Temple, a Reform synagogue in Brooklyn, New York, welcomes into their space a progressive minyan called Shir HaMa'alot. The minyan does not pay rent, but they do contribute a modest fee for maintenance. While some of the institutions that have come together in a community campus have not previously collaborated, the shrinking membership of these synagogues and their large physical plants have made such relationships possible and mutually beneficial.

Mergers

While a growing number of synagogues and other institutions are merging in the Jewish community, the community campus model is more about collaboration—a value increasingly upheld in both the for-profit and the not-for-profit community sectors—than merger. Still, some community campuses are the result of synagogue mergers. Such was the case with Temple Beth El (Reform) and Congregation Eilat (Conservative) in Orange County, California. Congregation Eilat was losing members and couldn't afford their mortgage, so their leaders asked the leaders of Beth El "to let them in," according to Rabbi Peter Levi, the spiritual leader of Beth El. The merged community has two sanctuaries and two kitchens (one kosher, one not kosher).

Not all community campus projects in the Jewish community include only Jewish institutions. For example, JCCs and YMCAs have merged. The first such arrangement—in Edison, New Jersey, in 2002—involved the JCC of Middlesex County and the local branch of the YMCA. This merger has allowed joint ownership of a facility, including a fitness center and swimming pool (the largest space in the building), in a catchment area with a limited local Jewish population, although surrounding areas have robust Jewish communities.

Makom Hadash

New York, New York

Established by Hazon (a Jewish organization dedicated to preserving the environment) in 2010, Makom Hadash is an innovative urban form of the more traditional campus model in that it occupies a suite of offices rather than a building. According to the website:

> Makom Hadash is a hub for the Jewish innovation community in New York, and a residency center for second-stage Jewish nonprofit organizations [those that are beyond the start-up phase but are not quite established]. Combining affordable space and office services with community and opportunities to learn, socialize and collaborate, it enables its member organizations to focus more on their missions, develop more sophisticated organizational infrastructure and collaborate more effectively together. Its programs offer networking, professional development, and opportunities for partnership to a range of smaller Jewish organizations and innovative programs.[2]

Makom Hadash "offers both reserved office spaces and flexible-hours arrangements. Organizations based outside of New York can join to use hot-desks, office services, and meeting spaces, and to connect with Jewish nonprofit colleagues."[3] Its programs are open to staff members of organizations with offices at Makom Hadash, as well as others in the so-called Jewish innovation sector. Ten organizations, including Hazon, have offices at Makom Hadash. While there are no synagogues involved in Makom Hadash, synagogues can learn from the model.

Shalom Park

Charlotte, North Carolina

The shared fifty-four-acre campus called Shalom Park, founded in 1986, was established to house both recreational and educational programs and facilities. Later it grew to include Temple Beth El

(Reform) and Temple Israel (Conservative), a Jewish Community Center, a Jewish Federation, and a community Jewish day school and preschool. Thus, institutions enjoy some economy of scale, although most of them maintain traditional membership or financial models. Facilities may be rented by the public. The Foundation of Shalom Park was established as the independent owner and manager of the facilities there. However, the two synagogues on the property operate independently from one another and from the foundation.

Asper Jewish Community Campus

Winnipeg, Manitoba, Canada

As with Shalom Park, an independent corporation was created as landlord for the Asper Jewish Community Campus, and all institutions are treated equally—that is, no one institution, including the Jewish Federation, has priority over the use of the facilities. Located on the former Fort Osborne Barracks and Agricultural College, the campus—which opened in 1997—consists of a 250,000-square-foot building. Like Shalom Park, it makes its shared facilities available for rental to the community. However, unlike Shalom Park, no synagogues have chosen to relocate to the Winnipeg facility.

Center for Jewish Life

Kingston, Pennsylvania

In Wilkes-Barre, Pennsylvania, a once-robust Jewish community that has seen recent decline is in the process of locating all of their community agencies, including two synagogues and a new Jewish Community Center, to one central location in Kingston, Pennsylvania. Proponents believe that developing a new campus will cost individual institutions less than making repairs to aging facilities. They also believe that participants will enjoy significant ongoing cost savings in a shared space. The Jewish communal leaders in Wilkes-Barre contend that the window of opportunity for this transition is rapidly closing. Should the community institutions not make the move soon, all of them will fail.

North Shore Congregation Israel

Glencoe, Illinois ▣ Reform ▣ Large

Some institutions have maintained a traditional membership model and rented to other institutions. North Shore Congregation Israel (NSCI) in Glencoe, Illinois, rents facilities to Aitz Hayim Center for Jewish Living (independent), which calls itself "a different kind of synagogue." While Aitz Hayim maintains a traditional model of membership, the children of Aitz Hayim members may attend the NSCI religious school and pay the same tuition costs as do members of NSCI. Some adult education programs are also shared. Until recently, NSCI also rented space to B'nai Torah (Reform) and ran a collaborative religious school with them, but unfortunately B'nai Torah was forced to close.

Congregation Beth Elohim

Brooklyn, New York ▣ Reform ▣ Large

Similarly, Congregation Beth Elohim (also known as Garfield Temple) in Brooklyn, New York, a Reform congregation founded in 1861 that maintains a classic membership model, hosts the group Brooklyn Jews in their large facility. The latter was an independent organization founded by Beth Elohim's current rabbi, Andy Bachman, prior to his joining Beth Elohim. Once at Beth Elohim, he invited Brooklyn Jews to become part of Beth Elohim, and that group became the outreach arm of the synagogue. Those who are involved in Brooklyn Jews can join Beth Elohim for a modest annual fee or simply remain as part of Brooklyn Jews without joining Beth Elohim.

The Altshul minyan (traditional, egalitarian, although independent) can best be described as a co-op. They have met at Congregation Beth Elohim for about ten years at no charge. Beth Elohim also serves as the minyan's fiscal sponsor. Minyan participants are encouraged but not required to join Congregation Beth Elohim, at a discounted level called Amit (Hebrew for colleague or friend). (See chapter 10 for more about the Altshul minyan.)

Both NSCI and Beth Elohim are ripe for the full community campus model and have already taken the foundational steps to adopt it.

North Shore Congregation Israel's Purpose

North Shore Congregation Israel's Purpose (according to its bylaws):

> North Shore Congregation Israel (in Hebrew: Adat Yisrael) is established, in the spirit of Reform Judaism, as a house of worship, study, and assembly in the service of God, of Torah and of the People Israel. We are committed to expressing our Jewish values by promoting active participation by all members in all areas of congregational life, and reclaiming spirituality within an evolving Jewish tradition.

In accordance with that purpose, NSCI will continue to be a congregation dedicated to the spiritual fulfillment of its members. We will value religious observance enhanced by *tikkun olam* (our obligation to repair the world), intellectual challenge, lifelong Jewish learning, and inspiring worship. Our welcoming community will nurture personal connections through Judaism, Jewish engagement and active participation in vibrant synagogue life....

Throughout the ages, the synagogue has served as the anchor and, in many ways, the center and sustainer of Jewish life. At this critical juncture, not only in our own synagogue's life, but in the shifting reality of Jewish identity and practice among the mainstream Jewish population in America, we at NSCI intend to continue to fulfill our mission, not only maintaining our important role as a vital and strong synagogue, but to optimize our reach, both within our established community and outside our walls, in both traditional and innovative ways.

"NSCI Strategic Direction Committee, Final Report, June 2, 2014," North Shore Congregation Israel website, https://nsci.org/sites/default/files/uploaded_documents/nsci_strategic_direction_committee_-_final_report.pdf.

Tri-Faith Initiative

Omaha, Nebraska

In the recently inaugurated Tri-Faith Initiative in Omaha, Nebraska, three faith groups have put down roots on a thirty-seven-acre tract of land once owned by a Jewish country club that closed once Jews were permitted to join the local country club. The Tri-Faith Initiative began as an attempt by Temple Israel (Reform), whose facility was near congested downtown Omaha, to find additional parking. Once the congregation decided to move the entire facility to West Omaha, Temple Israel's leaders became aware of a new mosque exploring building in the same area. The two groups approached the local Catholic Diocese to join their project. After the Catholic church expressed a lack of interest in the project, the group found a willing partner in the local Episcopal Diocese. The latter invited the Evangelical Lutheran church to join them in building a church. As of this writing, the Episcopal church has pulled out, but the

---

Founding Principles of the Tri-Faith Initiative

Looking for Shared Space Opportunities

- To the extent each Participant can agree to do so, they will create "shared space" that will allow for efficiencies of common operation and facilitate collaboration and interaction between and among the Participants.
- This is expected to include such basic things as parking and common outdoor areas.
- It is hoped to include such things as shared library space, food service, meeting rooms, auditorium, conference and banquet facilities and other common indoor areas.
- Unfunded costs to build and operate shared space shall be fairly allocated among Participants.

The Desire to Find Commonality

- Participants shall foster among their members an environment of acceptance, respect and trust-building towards other Participants and their members.

- Participants agree to seek and create opportunities for communities, groups, families and individuals to gather, meet, interact and learn about and from one another.
- Participants shall look for opportunities to understand differences and build on commonalities among Participants.
- A common "look and feel" shall be sought in the design of buildings on this campus.

Oversight and Governance of Common Areas

- Participants will cooperate to discuss and establish rules governing the Common/Shared spaces.
- This may be by direct establishment of an organization to do so, in which event each Participant shall have equal voice.
- It may be by delegation of such responsibilities to a third party organization, but only by consent of all Participants.
- Rules governing shared space and practices allowed therein will give maximum consideration to issues of respect for and tolerance of the beliefs of all Participants.
- When conflicts arise, Participants agree to engage in open discussions, with sensitivity to all other Participants, to work in good faith and exercise their best efforts to amicably resolve such conflicts.
- Additional Participants may be welcomed upon (unanimous) agreement of each of the Participants.
- Clergy of Participants shall be encouraged to meet and agree upon additional and more specific rules and guidelines for use of such common space.

Vision Statement

In working together, our vision is to build bridges of respect, trust and acceptance, to challenge stereotypes of each other, to learn from one another, and to counter the influence of extremists and agents of hate.

Tri-Faith Initiative, "Memorandum of Understanding," November 2006, http://trifaith.org/?page_id=677.

United Church of Christ has become interested in participating in the project. The original partnership was formed in 2006, but the first building didn't open until 2013. Each group is responsible for purchasing land and building their own facility. Together, the Tri-Faith Initiative will build the fourth building on the property for the purpose of interfaith collaboration. It is too early to determine whether this project will impact the membership or dues structure of the synagogue or will represent an economy-of-scale savings. Nonetheless, it is a noteworthy project.

Genesis of Ann Arbor

Ann Arbor, Michigan

Genesis of Ann Arbor took a different development path. On Packard Road, passersby see a cross and a Star of David standing next to one another, to represent the corporation that was created by St. Clare of Assisi Episcopal Church and Temple Beth Emeth (Reform).

The Special Nature of Genesis of Ann Arbor

Genesis of Ann Arbor represents a special relationship between an Episcopal church and a Reform Jewish temple wherein both congregations maintain their separate ethnic identities to worship and be fruitful in the ways that are unique to both understandings of the nature of God. This relationship stands as a symbol of the power of reason and love to overcome distrust and the prejudices of our separate histories.

The facilities of Genesis are intended to serve the sacred as well as the special needs of each congregation. Implicit in the shared use is a recognition of responsibilities to serve the broader Ann Arbor community, making available its facilities for purposes consonant with the values and principles of Genesis. All users of the space are expected to recognize the special nature of the Genesis arrangement and to use the premises gently.

Genesis of Ann Arbor website, www.genesisa2.org/Genesis/Genesis_-_Facility_Use.html.

These institutions formed the corporation in 1974 to own, operate, and maintain the shared facilities. Each congregation maintains their own identity, but representatives of both participate on the Genesis board. Several times a year, especially on civil holidays, the two congregations host joint programs. Each congregation also maintains their own approach to membership.

Congregation Kehillah

Scottsdale, Arizona ▣ Independent ▣ Small

Numerous synagogues have developed a variety of relationships with churches. Often, they share parking lots and other facilities that are in proximity to both institutions, and a few share sacred spaces. Congregation Kehillah (founded in 2008) moved to Via de Cristo United Methodist Church (VDC) in Scottsdale, Arizona. VDC was looking for an institutional partner of a different faith with shared values, and Congregation Kehillah was looking for new space. While both institutions remain independent, their collaboration is built around their work in the area of social justice.

Kadima

Canton, Ohio

More similar to the community campus model is Kadima in Canton, Ohio. Canton's Jewish community was once thriving and robust, independent of those in nearby Akron and Cleveland. With the economic decline of America's Rust Belt, Jewish businesses closed, and community members, particularly the adult children of local residents, moved away. Canton had little new commerce to draw people to the community. Eventually, community leaders formed the Gesher (literally, bridge) strategic planning group, bringing together members of the Reform (Temple Israel) and Conservative (Shaaray Torah Synagogue) synagogues and the remaining community agencies in an attempt to efficiently utilize resources. The extent of their early successes was evidenced in a joint religious school for the Reform and Conservative synagogues called Chadash (literally, new), established in 2006. The school has one director and meets at Temple Israel.

With the establishment of Chadash, the Gesher project evolved into Kadima (literally, advance or forward), with committees and discussions that focused on religious, legal, financial, and facilities issues for an eventual merger of the institutions or physical plants. In 2012 Temple Israel and the Jewish Federation/Jewish Community Center moved into the Shaaray Torah Synagogue, which was refurbished to meet the needs of all three institutions, now called Beit Ha'am (House of the People). The three institutions' buildings were already located next to one another, and Shaaray Torah seemed best suited to accommodate the needs of all three. Relocating to the Shaaray Torah facility was also the least costly option. Following the trend in many communities, the JCC had already been taken over by the Jewish Federation and became the Federation's program arm.

While the institutions share space, the Reform community continues to be led by a full-time rabbi and cantorial soloist, and the Conservative community continues to be led by a full-time cantor and part-time (visiting) rabbi. Also now on the premises is the local Anglo-Jewish newspaper (*The Stark Jewish News*), a sanctuary, a smaller worship space, a reference and research library, and some classrooms. The library is open to the public. The refurbished building also has a small apartment for visiting rabbis (for the Conservative synagogue) who don't drive on Shabbat and two kitchens (one kosher, one not).

Kol Yisrael

Newburgh, New York

In Newburgh, New York, as in Canton, Ohio, two congregations are now sharing a building overseen by a joint operations board. Temple Beth Jacob (Reform) sold their building to join Congregation Agudas Israel (Conservative) and the local Jewish Community Center in the refurbished Agudas Israel building. The new building is named Kol Yisrael. The various spaces will be used to accommodate the worship needs of both institutions. In addition, the JCC provides programs for the children of both synagogues.

Dell Jewish Community Campus

Austin, Texas

While many communities look toward the community campus model as a way to save money and avoid duplicating resources, the Dell Jewish Community Campus in Austin, Texas, was established not primarily for those reasons, but from a position of fiscal health and the belief that creating a community campus is valuable. With the strong support of communal leaders, the community came together to create a center of Jewish life and living. Since the 1970s Austin had had a small community campus where some communal institutions were located, so the notion of a community campus was familiar to the community and valued by it. A gift of the former Hart Family Ranch by Michael and Susan Dell in 1992 made a real campus possible, and it opened in 2000. The Jewish Community Association of Austin serves as the umbrella organization for the campus, with three main divisions: JCC, Jewish Federation, and Jewish Family Service. These divisions are separate from the synagogues, but they do provide services to the synagogues' constituencies. The forty-acre campus plays host to Reform, Conservative, and Orthodox synagogues, as well as independent minyanim, the Austin Jewish Academy, the Jewish Community Center, and nearly the entire organizational structure of the community.

Highlights

The community campus model is desirable because it has the potential to fully utilize the available space in a synagogue. The community campus gives organizations a way to more efficiently utilize resources and brings various elements of the community together in the same location. The economic benefits may even serve as a motive for this model's implementation. By employing this model, synagogue leaders are able to accomplish two important things. First, the plan enables leaders to bring to the synagogue those in the Jewish community who may participate in other activities and not yet be engaged in the synagogue. Second, it helps leaders bring to synagogue members services that might otherwise be provided elsewhere. Rather than operating just as a landlord, synagogue leaders have the opportunity to use their real estate thoughtfully, bringing together resources that serve the membership of the synagogue and yet are beyond the services the synagogue provides.

1. All tenants on a community campus should be equal.
2. An independent corporation is established to maintain the campus.

Frequently Asked Questions

Challengers to the community campus model may be fearful of losing their personal history with the sacred space of their synagogue, especially if creating a campus involves relocation or reconstruction, as it often does. Thus, it will be important for campus designers to highlight the history of any predecessor institutions by maintaining ritual items, donor plaques, and memorial boards. Similarly, to ensure the success of the new model, synagogue leaders must find ways to celebrate the new direction of the synagogue and at the same time demonstrate the continuity of past to present to future.

Does a synagogue have to be large and have a large physical plant to implement the community campus model?

While a larger institution might more easily and productively implement this model, any size congregation can do so. For the most part, larger institutions have higher overhead and more unused and underutilized space.

What kinds of organizations are best suited to reside on the community campus?

Those institutions and organizations whose missions resonate with the synagogue or that can provide relevant services to its members are best suited to join the campus. Such institutions and organizations should not be limited to those affiliated with the Jewish community, however. For example, a synagogue that is interested in contemplative practices may welcome a yoga studio to its facility.

Implementation Steps

Step 1. Consider the other synagogues and Jewish institutions in your community. Which ones might be interested in joining you on your campus or relocating together to a new, neutral site? Will resources be used more efficiently as a result? Will the facility be more centrally located? If so, will that location benefit member organizations?

Step 2. Now consider other organizations or institutions in your community that are not Jewish—perhaps including mosques and churches, as well as other religious organizations—but whose ideology is resonant with that of your synagogue. Which ones might be interested in joining you on your campus or relocating together to a new, neutral site?

Step 3. Convene leaders from the relevant institutions and organizations. Determine whether you are to become a landlord, the institutions will merge, or the partners will together develop a campus. Together decide how membership in the campus will function. In other words, will people be members of specific institutions or of the entire campus community?

Step 4. Develop a budget for the campus. Consider which spaces will be shared and which spaces will be private, that is, available for use by an individual institution. Identify any cost savings for administrative overhead, group buying, and shared spaces. This should be shared with the board leadership responsible for budget and future planning.

Step 5. Work with partner institutions to develop the campus and coordinate outreach efforts.

Notes for Adapting This Model for Our Synagogue

When there is no vision, the people perish.

Proverbs 29:18

I want to be a part of a synagogue because I want to be a part of the Jewish people, and there is no other institution that unites the Jews as well, across the centuries and across the borders. The synagogue is not only a bond to my past. It is also a bond to the Jewish people of the present, the ones with whom I live. During the week, I may bump into them somewhere, as a neighbor, as a friend, as a client, perhaps even as a co-worker or as a competitor. But when we meet together in this place, we meet as partners. We stand here with a sense of being connected to each other, and of being responsible for each other.

Rabbi Jack Reimer[1]

10

The Co-op Model

The International Cooperative Alliance (ICA) defines a co-op as "an autonomous association of persons who voluntarily cooperate for their mutual social, economic, and cultural benefit." The ICA's definition makes the translation of this model into the synagogue setting easy to see. Although the co-op model extends to housing, utilities, banking, and other arenas, it is particularly popular in the agriculture and food industry—groceries, farms, and meat- and wine-buying groups. Within these settings, members of the co-op are given specific so-called sweat equity responsibilities. These responsibilities usually require a time commitment and might take advantage of the particular skills of an individual. A food co-op might require its members to be available to receive produce or stock its shelves during the hours when the co-op is open, for example. For some co-ops, this responsibility may be required in addition to membership dues. In most cases, however, the sweat equity replaces dues but is required of all members. Such an approach in the synagogue allows members to pay dues totally in the form of volunteer work or partially through work and the remainder with a standard financial payment.

The volunteer work is designed to mitigate the costs of overhead for maintaining the institution and lower costs for members. The co-op model thereby addresses the revenue needs of a synagogue by eliminating many expenses. The members of the co-op synagogue gain a sense of ownership over the institution and can feel proud that they built and continue to expand and maintain it.

The Kavana Cooperative

Seattle, Washington ▣ Independent ▣ Small

The primary example of a synagogue that uses the co-op membership model is the Kavana Cooperative, led by Rabbi Rachel Nussbaum. The Kavana Cooperative identifies itself as "the first Jewish cooperative of its kind," where "partners share in the task of creating Jewish life for the group." This group life could include prayer, adult or family learning, home observance, community involvement, a book group, Jewish cooking, or something else. This co-op considers itself nondenominational and pluralistic. Their leaders believe that their approach to Jewish life helps their members personalize their Judaism in a community context. Moreover, the Kavana Cooperative claims to "draw participants from highly diverse backgrounds and provide for multiple entry points to Jewish involvement," while "acknowledg[ing] and embrac[ing] the dynamic tension between an individual's interest and needs, versus the desire to create community." Finally, this co-op believes "that Jewish communal life will best thrive in settings which are local, organic and intimate."[2]

The Kavana Cooperative refers to their members as partners. While an individual need not be a partner to participate in the community, the Kavana Cooperative does expect regular participants to become partners. The benefits of partnership are quite similar to those of a general synagogue member: access to clergy for life-cycle events, participation in leadership, discounts on fees. The Kavana Cooperative also expects their partners to contribute both time and money, noting that "the amount of time and money a partner contributes varies proportionally to the depth and duration of their involvement in the community." In the end, "Kavana is a cooperative, and to work it presumes a meaningful volunteer commitment from all partner households."[3] While anyone is welcome to participate in Kavana events, only partners may vote and are privy to what might otherwise be considered private information, such as the financial records of the cooperative. Since Kavana rents their space, there are no building fund requirements of their partners. Tuition for various educational programs, such as the middle school program recommended for bar/bat mitzvah students, is an additional cost to partners. Partners are charged $18 per High Holy Day ticket; others are charged $180 per ticket, but no one is turned away because of an inability to pay.

Jewish Collaborative of San Diego

San Diego, California ▣ Independent ▣ Small

As a self-described "cooperative-inspired synagogue community,"[4] the Jewish Collaborative of San Diego (JCoSD) seeks to empower their membership to determine the direction the congregation should be headed. "Cooperative" for JCoSD means that "most of [the] activities, events, and programs will be inspired, designed, written, and facilitated by the members of [the] community." As stated in the description of their mission, "The JCoSD organizes along lines of interest and inspiration," rather than demographic lines. For the JCoSD, collaboration includes financial and human resources. However, family members are asked to pay up to 1 percent of their annual income or $1,500 a year. Members are given the right to "vote on all issues that affect them directly." Since the members of JCoSD understand themselves as "a community structured in the cooperative model," their leaders feel that members should be able to determine what applies and appeals to them within the congregation. Members are empowered to partner with synagogue leadership "to create the ritual experience that best matches who [they] are, and what [they] stand for."[5] JCoSD has yet to establish a religious school or building, but members are given priority to participate in what they call a High Holy Day "experience."

Altshul

Brooklyn, New York ▣ Independent ▣ Small

The Altshul minyan was founded in 2005 by about twenty-five people who wanted to establish a traditional worship experience that is egalitarian (where men and women are equal and no class distinctions are made). The founders sought to create a worship community in Brooklyn that is guided by Jewish law, rather than personal, intuitive decisions. Altshul has no rabbi, although they do consult with Rabbi Ethan Tucker of Mechon Hadar if any Jewish legal issues need to be decided. The group also has no president. Originally, a

Volunteering at Altshul

Altshul runs entirely on volunteer power. From setting up and leading services, to sponsoring kiddush, organizing Kindershul [children's service], or hosting a social event, the community thrives because people pitch in to make it happen.

To keep things running smoothly, and enable people to pitch in, all regular Altshul participants are asked to volunteer to set up and clean up on one Shabbat morning or one Friday night each year. Volunteers are supported with easy-to-follow instructions and a teammate.

"Volunteer!," Altshul website, www.altshul.org/participate/ways/.

steering committee coordinated all programs and services. In 2012, Altshul changed their structure, so an overall leadership team oversees teams that handle various aspects of the minyan. These teams are what make Altshul a co-op, since all of the members participate in them. When any question arises, the team makes decisions for the minyan; thus, their members do not have voting rights. The Atlshul minyan meets at Congregation Beth Elohim in Brooklyn (see chapter 9 for more details about their arrangement). There are no membership dues for Altshul; however, members of the minyan are given a discounted rate for membership at their host synagogue—Congregation Beth Elohim—with all attendant benefits of membership there. Life-cycle events are handled both within the context of the minyan and at Congregation Beth Elohim, depending on the nature of the event and the number of guests attending. The individual or family member is responsible for any relevant fees, including tutoring costs if any are incurred.

Highlights

The co-op model is important because it values the labor of individuals as much as it does financial support for the synagogue. The co-op model is also familiar to—and currently in vogue with—many people, who may even participate in other co-ops, such as a day-care or food co-op. With a co-op, volunteerism, a lost value and activity in large segments of the community, can once again become a community value.

1. The co-op model addresses some of the revenue needs of a synagogue by eliminating some expenses through the volunteer work required of its members.
2. Members may be required to make a financial contribution to the community, or they may instead contribute in the form of "sweat equity."

Frequently Asked Questions

One of the challenges in all co-ops is that everyone has an equal voice in leadership and responsibility and may try to exert that leadership over the institution. This can lead to "too many generals, not enough privates," as the saying goes. However, when people feel that they own something—even cooperatively—they take successes and failures far more personally. They are more invested in the future of the institution as well.

If a synagogue co-op does not require an access fee and requires only sweat equity, does that prevent hiring professional staff and having a building?

Yes. Either the synagogue has to determine another alternative revenue stream, or it would have to require all "staff," as members of the co-op, to volunteer their time without financial compensation. In other words, all traditional staff functions would be carried out by volunteers. In this way, either the synagogue is led by (lay) volunteer leaders, or the rabbi is also a co-op member who is not paid a salary.

Is there a point when the synagogue co-op becomes too large?

Yes. When the synagogue no longer feels like an intimate group where all members know each other, the co-op might need to split into multiple communities.

Implementation Steps

Step 1. Identify the sweat equity opportunities in the synagogue. Ask, in what ways can a person volunteer to eliminate expenses for the synagogue?

Step 2. Divide the total expenses identified in step 1 by the number of potential households to determine your access/cooperative fee (dues), if these will be charged.

Step 3. Motivate volunteer leaders who will manage the cooperative enterprise and other volunteers.

Step 4. Develop and roll out marketing materials that reflect the new membership model. Include personal narratives of partners/owners about their role in the co-op and how they and their families benefit from participation in it.

Notes for Adapting This Model for Our Synagogue

Even in Paradise, it is not good to be alone.

Yiddish proverb

We also must understand that no two organizations are exactly alike and no two synagogues share exactly the same issues. While there are issues that all congregations share, there are also significant ways they differ.

Rabbi Randall J. Konigsburg[1]

11

The Hybrid Model

As mentioned previously, although synagogues are similar in many ways, no two synagogues—or communities—are alike. The variety explains why some communities may think they cannot adopt a new model in its entirety. For example, a synagogue in the New York City area may approach the open membership model differently from a synagogue in Tuscaloosa, Alabama, since there are so many synagogues in New York City and there is only one synagogue in Tuscaloosa. But synagogues may be able to combine elements of several to create a hybrid model. In music, the result is called a mash-up. It takes the best elements of the various songs and creates a better version by combining them. Sometimes it is the combination of the two songs that makes the finished tune more interesting. When dealing with two pieces of equal value, the mash-up often increases the musical impact of both.

Elements to Consider in Creating a Hybrid Model

To determine which of the elements of a particular model work for your synagogue, consider the following:

How large is the local Jewish population?

If the Jewish population in a particular area is small and the expenses for a congregation are large, then contributions from that small population may not suffice. On the other hand, if the community is large and dispersed, then trying to appeal to and accommodate everyone may not be realistic.

How many area synagogues are there in your catchment area?

Unfortunately, synagogues often view their neighboring institutions as competition. From a financial standpoint, that could be the case. However, the acknowledgment of competition from other institutions might force synagogues to better clarify their missions, especially in comparison to one another.

How long has your synagogue been in existence?

Synagogues with a long-standing congregational history may have a low level of risk tolerance. Yet these congregations may be the most in need of change. Young synagogues may also be risk averse, because they are not firmly established in the community. Before making any changes, an institution should determine its risk tolerance.

What is the future membership trajectory of your synagogue?

Consider the demographics of the synagogue's surrounding area. Are people moving into your community—for work, the neighborhood, schooling, your synagogue? Can the synagogue encourage people to move into its local area? Which models might work best to attract people?

Congregation Dorshei Tzedek

West Newton, Massachusetts ▣ Reconstructionist ▣ Small

Congregation Dorshei Tzedek took elements from the minimal dues (close to no-dues), fair share, and voluntary dues models to shape their hybrid. The members of Dorshei Tzedek pride themselves on being "dedicated to Jewish learning and to ethical Jewish living in the modern world."[2] As a result, the synagogue grounds their membership system on Jewish biblical tradition and history. Each adult member of the synagogue is assessed a symbolic "half shekel" of $125, a base payment for membership; as noted in chapter 1, the half shekel was a Temple (Tabernacle) tax. Members then determine their gross household income and pay dues, based on a sliding scale, of approximately 1.0 to 1.6 percent of their income. The continuing challenge for Congregation Dorshei Tzedek is that the base half shekel and the self-assessment do not provide enough funds to sustain the institution; thus, they require additional financial support beyond dues. Each member of the congregation is therefore expected to make an additional voluntary contribution of an amount "that is right for them" (Exodus 25:2). These contributions are referred to as *Nediv Lev* contributions—voluntary donations from the heart. High Holy Day tickets are included in membership, but religious school tuition is extra. Members of the synagogue have voting rights. Since Dorshei Tzedek has no building, there are no building fund obligations for members.

The Community Synagogue

Port Washington, New York ▣ Reform ▣ Medium

Like many synagogues that have adopted and adapted new models for membership and funding, The Community Synagogue has employed their own hybrid. On the surface, it appears as if The Community Synagogue uses a fair share dues plan—each member family unit paying dues to the synagogue according to its ability. Each family unit "assesses itself according to six broad income categories."[3] This defines a dues bracket (think tax bracket) that allows families to avoid disclosing the specifics of their income. New members may either pay only half dues or participate in The Community Synagogue's "gift membership program," which allows new members to join at no cost for the first year (excluding *b'nai mitzvah*). High Holy Day tickets and *b'nai mitzvah* training are included in membership dues at the synagogue, but religious school fees are additional. All members of the synagogue have voting rights.

Sha'ar Communities

Northern New Jersey ▣ Independent ▣ Small

Sha'ar (literally, gate) Communities in Northern New Jersey has implemented a prime example of a hybrid system. According to their founder, Rabbi Adina Lewittes, Sha'ar Communities has established two options for associating with the synagogue: membership and fee-for-service. Membership is a typical comprehensive fee for those who want to avail themselves of the full array of programming and opportunities available. Some offerings may be open to nonmembers, but members are privileged in various ways, as might be expected: reduced program fees, access to events, leadership opportunities, and access to clergy for life-cycle events. Potential members also have the opportunity to join a particular *sha'ar* or gate, rather than the entirety of Sha'ar Communities, at a lower cost.

Those who don't want to join Sha'ar as full members through one of the gates are offered the opportunity to choose among the various aspects of Jewish communal life and to pay accordingly for specific programs or services. Members can also join one of the communities and gain access to all the benefits of that particular community. The synagogue offers six different communities, or "gates." The Gate of Prayer offers music-filled Shabbat and holiday services. The Gate of Study provides weekly classes. The Gate of Tomorrow contains educational programs for youth. The Gate of Repair is for those who are interested in multigenerational social justice activities. The Gate of Discovery focuses on educational experiences through travel. The Gate of Healing and Wholeness contains ritual and spiritual fellowship for those who are experiencing change and transition. A web-based effort, Sha'ar's newest gate is the Virtual Gate, which is specifically for those who do not live in Northern New Jersey, where Sha'ar is located.

For Rabbi Lewittes, this decentralized model addresses several rising trends: people want the opportunity to choose and control the content of their Jewish lives; flexibility and fluidity with regard to membership in Jewish institutions; smaller, intimate communities, rather than larger, formal settings; and an affordable path to living Jewishly. Single, comprehensive, and expensive membership dues are replaced with individual (or multiple) targeted and affordable payments for selected areas of involvement. No formal or overall membership is needed to enjoy access to programs, events, or mission-specific communities. Leadership opportunities (and expectations) are made available to every participant, and spiritual guidance is provided to each community. It is also important to note that Sha'ar Communities has no building, consistent with their philosophical approach to fostering a synagogue community without the financial burden of a physical structure. A building also may limit where events and ceremonies might take place. But Lewittes believes that the model can be applied to synagogues that occupy a building.

The Community Free Synagogue

Fort Myers, Florida ▣ Independent ▣ Medium

The Community Free Synagogue (CFS) is another example of a hybrid. However, the models CFS employs are different from those used by Sha'ar Communities. Founded in 2004 by Rabbi Bruce Diamond, CFS is a no-dues, no-fees synagogue that depends totally on voluntary contributions and the volunteer labors of their members. The synagogue does not hold fundraising events or solicit pledges, nor do they charge for youth education, *b'nai mitvah*, Passover seders, High Holy Day services, and the like. However, the synagogue does use online crowdfunding to generate a significant portion of their budget. CFS even avoids the term "member" and uses the term "participant" instead. Over 400 households now consider themselves part of the Community Free Synagogue. The most recent Passover included two free community seders, which were attended by over 300 people, and over 1,500 people attended CFS High Holy Day services. The synagogue's board includes only a president, vice president, and treasurer, which allows for a nearly entrepreneurial model, much like Chabad (mentioned in chapter 6). Thus, members of the board are the only ones with voting rights in the synagogue.

92nd Street Y

New York City

The 92nd Street Y, a well-known New York City institution, is not a synagogue. Nevertheless, it increasingly offers programs akin to those synagogues provide, such as a full range of Shabbat programming under the rubric Shababa (a play on the word "Shabbat" and *sababa,* which means "awesome"). The organization simultaneously uses a tiered membership model and a no-membership model. While most of its programs, especially its well-attended lectures and concerts, are open to the public without a membership, it also offers a health and fitness membership. Individuals can also take advantage of "Jewish Life-Cycle Coaching" on a transactional (fee-for-service) basis.

Highlights

The hybrid model provides the synagogue with numerous options for membership and dues restructuring, potentially avoiding the limitations of various models. Even within current structures, most synagogue leaders use a hybrid—a primary model supported by at least one secondary approach to membership. As a model, the hybrid provides the most flexibility of all of the membership models presented in this book. As a result, it is more of a strategic approach to membership and dues than an actual system. The hybrid model has the potential to constantly evolve and thus does not force the synagogue to maintain one model for an extended period of time. Rather, it allows the congregation to be nimble and respond rapidly to changes in the surrounding culture and environment.

1. No two synagogues are identical. Thus, they may need to use elements of the various models presented in this volume.
2. A hybrid could evolve into its own unique new model.
3. A synagogue conducts an internal evaluation to determine which hybrid best reflects their mission and responds to their financial challenges.

Frequently Asked Questions

There is no perfect hybrid formula for a synagogue. That fact alone may lead to second-guessing by critics who do not want to leave behind the traditional membership-and-dues model. While each synagogue is probably more like than unlike other synagogues, the hybrid addresses what is indeed unique to the individual synagogue. Synagogue leaders and change agents should be prepared to clearly articulate why they conceived the particular hybrid chosen for the synagogue and how it addresses the specific needs of their synagogue.

How will we know for sure which key elements will work for our synagogue?

There is no way to know for sure. Compare the needs of your synagogue to the examples described throughout this book, and then carefully choose those elements that address the challenges your congregation is facing.

What should we do if we are completely risk averse and therefore unable to make a decision about which model or elements of models to adopt?

To help minimize the risks—especially financial risks—find a group of people who may be willing to assist the congregation financially should the chosen hybrid fail.

At what point will we be able to determine that our transition has been successful?

Like other models, the hybrid addresses issues specific to a given congregation. Thus, each element has to be evaluated independently. Taking them together, you can determine the success of the transition if you have successfully replaced the current membership and revenue model without losing members or revenue.

Implementation Steps

Step 1. Identify which elements of your synagogue are the most successful and draw the most people.

Step 2. Break down your program into various service areas. Then identify which model will best address each component. One component does not have to be dominant.

Step 3. Communicate the new model to current members and to the community.

Notes for Adapting This Model for Our Synagogue

The Torah suggests that we were created to be in community, that only in community do we sense the presence of God, and that only in and through community can we become holy.

Carol Ochs[1]

There is a legend about the Temple that once stood in Jerusalem. It is about its windows. Ancient buildings like the castles and churches we visit throughout Europe constructed their windows so as to funnel the natural light from the outside in. In other words the windows cut into the building's thick stone walls were wider on the outside and thinner on the inside. The Temple's windows were the opposite. They were larger on the inside. Their purpose was to funnel the light from the inside to the outside, to bring the meaning and content gained within to the world at large. That is the purpose of the synagogue: to bring light to the outside, to build a fire together to warm the community. The purpose is to bring Torah to the world.

Rabbi Steven Moskowitz[2]

Conclusion

It's nearly impossible to consider alternative membership and revenue models for the synagogue without addressing some of the institutions that have emerged as alternatives to the synagogue. There is an increasing number of these institutions developing on the landscape of the American Jewish community. Many of them have been started by the millennial generation (those born between the early 1980s and the beginning of the twenty-first century) in an effort to meet the needs of their contemporaries. This tells us that this population is not as disinterested or as hard to reach as we are given to believe. It also tells us that their perception is that existing Jewish communal institutions have not made sufficient room for them—particularly in leadership roles—or that they simply don't resonate with the existing synagogue models.

While some of these new institutions already have been identified in this book, neither the independent minyan nor its impact has been fully explored. (For a full analysis of this movement, see Elie Kaunfer's *Empowered Judaism: What Independent Minyanim Can Teach Us about Building Vibrant Jewish Communities* [Jewish Lights].) Generally, the term "independent minyan" is used to describe any worship and study community that is led and organized by peers, rather than by rabbis, cantors, and other synagogue professionals. Strictly speaking, they are independent of any denomination, religious movement, or synagogue structure within the organized Jewish community.

Among the most well-known of these independent minyanim is Kehilat Hadar in New York City, defined as "an independent, egalitarian community committed to spirited traditional prayer, study and social action."[3] Formed in 2001 by Dr. Mara Benjamin, Rabbi Elie Kaunfer, and Rabbi Ethan Tucker while they were still graduate students, the minyan now meets for Shabbat morning services and some Friday nights; they also offer holiday services and educational programs throughout the year. The services are lively and engaging. Prayer leaders presume a considerable amount of literacy among participants, many of whom grew up in the various religious youth movements; thus, there are few "stage directions" during the service. A Torah teaching is offered, but no formal sermon is delivered.

Kehilat Hadar has no formal membership structure. Nevertheless, they do suggest annual individual contributions of $360 (or $240 for full-time students). They also have suggested donations for High Holy Day services. Moreover, those who donate are given discounted rates, which the minyan calls "preferential pricing," to participate in Kehilat Hadar's annual Shavuot retreat.

Mishkan Chicago: Who We Are

Mishkan is a burgeoning spiritual community in Chicago reclaiming Judaism's inspiration and transformative essence. Not bound by a particular location, we meet for soulful musical prayer and learning at homes and spaces all around the city, from synagogues to yoga studios.

The Torah describes the Mishkan as a tent that the ancient Israelites carried with them through the desert, creating holy space whenever and wherever they stopped to gather around and in it. Wherever we are on our journeys as Jews and as citizens of the world, we create meaningful connections—with ourselves, with others, with Jewish wisdom and with God—when we gather together in prayer, song, learning, and *tikkun* (repairing the world). That's what Mishkan is all about.

So join the rabbi for coffee, show up at a house party in your neighborhood, get inspired at a Friday night service, get involved in *tikkun* (repairing the world) work. Meet other folks in Chicago who are hungry for deeper Jewish experiences that get us higher, push us farther, and get us more and more connected.

"Who We Are," Mishkan Chicago website, www.mishkanchicago.org/who-we-are/.

Two of the original founders of Kehilat Hadar—Rabbi Ethan Tucker and Rabbi Elie Kaunfer—joined with Rabbi Shai Held (Kehilat Hadar's former scholar-in-residence) to form Mechon Hadar in 2006. The latter institution aims to revitalize prayer, study, and community life among young Jews in America, through Yeshivat Hadar (a full-time text study and social action program on the Upper West Side of Manhattan open to men and women) and the Minyan Project (education, consulting, and networking for prayer communities). While both institutions are independent of one another, they share the same vision for Jewish communal life. Moreover, the development of Kehilat Hadar informs the work of Mechon Hadar, especially as leaders of the latter institution work with and provide guidance to other independent minyanim thoughout North America.

While independent minyanim are still in their nascent stage of development in North America, they have the potential to be part of what has become known as disruptive innovation, something that has the potential to gradually undermine an entire system (or industry, in the commercial arena) without anyone fully realizing that such a change is taking place. Moreover, if these independent minyanim gain traction among the millennial generation and become their "go-to" place, they will displace more normative synagogue institutions. Independent minyanim also have the potential to force the American rabbinate from a professional model back into a vocational model—in which rabbis will have to make their living outside of the synagogue.

Other institutions have gone beyond the independent minyan model to create spiritual communities that transcend the worship experience. Because these communities have chosen alternative membership and revenue models, they are important to mention in this book. Mishkan Chicago, founded in 2011, is such an institution. Rabbi Lizzi Heydemann is the catalyst behind this spiritual community. Inspired by IKAR in Los Angeles and Congregation B'nai Jeshurun in New York City, she also sought to bring the music and meditation of South America into Mishkan Chicago. According to the Mishkan Chicago website, Rabbi Heydemann sees the need to create:

> Young, dynamic spiritual communities that resonate with the next generation, as well as people who have felt on the fringes of the Jewish community: queer Jews, people in interfaith relationships, spiritual seekers, Jews of color, Jews by choice. Mishkan was born out of, and seeks to fill, this gap on Chicago's spiritual landscape. If we're doing our job right, you will walk out of an experience at Mishkan knowing that Judaism is alive with Spirit, connection, spiritual and intellectual challenge, and moral awakening.[4]

Everyone is welcome at Mishkan Chicago, irrespective of their financial ability. Rather than refer to Mishkan participants as members, Mishkan uses the term "builders"—a reference to those who build the Mishkan community. Builders are given a variety of benefits, including priority to High Holy Day services, although everyone is welcome to attend; life-cycle events are available only to builders. There is no building fund obligation. Decisions about Mishkan are left to professional leadership and, on occasion, presented to the board, which includes Rabbi Heydemann. Builders are not included in the decision-making process.

Other Emerging Synagogue Models

While there are many possibilities to consider when making changes to your synagogue's membership and revenue model, we have included only ten full-scale models in this book. Nevertheless, you might want to take other steps to enhance any membership or revenue model currently in place in your synagogue. While the following are not fully developed membership models, they may supplement most of the models already described in this book. All of them have the potential to reach a larger target population and increase your revenue and participation.

Lifetime Memberships

A lifetime membership is an opportunity for an individual or a household to make a substantial onetime payment to the synagogue in return for membership benefits of which the member can take advantage throughout his or her life. Family benefits may be included.

Legacy Memberships

Similar to the lifetime membership, a legacy membership allows an individual or a household to make a substantial onetime payment to the synagogue in return for lifetime membership for one's descendants. The number of successive generations that can take advantage of this membership will be determined by the amount of the legacy membership payment.

Synagogue as a Cause

Many synagogues have strong social justice programs, some so strong that they attract people to the synagogue simply to participate in it. Some synagogues with urban roots, such as Central Reform Congregation in St. Louis, Missouri, have returned to the city to emphasize the social justice role of the synagogue in their neighborhood. Their role was particularly apparent during the riots in nearby Ferguson, Missouri, in summer 2014. Although few synagogues are actually built around a single mission, particularly social justice, synagogue communities can build their institution entirely around a specific cause. Members form an affinity group around the issue and raise funds to address it. Synagogues may also want to borrow from other institutions that consider themselves alternatives to synagogues, as mentioned above.

Minimal Dues

Some Jewish Community Centers have opted to charge members very modest minimal dues and then charge fees for all programs. Minimal dues in the synagogue would have to be supplemented by an extensive fundraising program. This approach, advocated for synagogues by Rabbi Gil Student, reflects the model used by Orthodox synagogues that auction Torah honors and the like. He also believes that this approach must be accompanied by requests for the funding of specific programs throughout the year. He contends that this will keep the dues low and still allow the synagogue to operate. The Isaac Agree Downtown Synagogue in Detroit, Michigan, charges dues of as little as $18 per year and offers free High Holy Day services to anyone. There are no building fund requirements, and the synagogue charges fees for their various programs and activities as needed. All members enjoy full voting rights in the synagogue.

The Boutique Synagogue

The boutique synagogue is modeled on the private synagogue, usually built by a wealthy individual or a community association, in Germany and elsewhere in Europe, and on the growing crop of boutique physician practices (sometimes referred to as concierge medicine) in the United States. In a boutique medical practice, the patient pays an annual fee, similar to a retainer for services, to the primary care physician. In return for the retainer, the physician provides the patient with enhanced personal care, as well as a commitment to limit the size of the medical practice to make sure that the physician is always available to the patient when needed and that the patient can make an appointment promptly and does not have to wait at the physician's office. There are a few contemporary private synagogues, such as the one built and owned by Ron Perelman in New York City, a small one-room brick structure between the two townhouses he owns on Manhattan's Upper East Side. Synagogues that have limited their memberships are, in a sense, following the boutique model. Members pay a specific amount for dues and limit the size of the synagogue's membership. The limiting of membership is not restricted to small, boutique synagogues. Up until 2014, Central Synagogue in New York City, a large Reform synagogue of 2,300 families, placed a cap on membership. At that time, they accepted those who were on the waiting list and then closed membership once again.

The Time-Share Model

While readers might consider the time-share model the most radical of the ideas in this book and therefore the least likely to be attempted, we describe it because it provides members with the opportunity to wholly own the synagogue. This allows members to completely control the institution and its direction. Congregants would pay for a share of the total value of the synagogue and then pay an annual fee to maintain the institution. The cost of a share amount would be determined by the number of projected members and the total value of the institution. Some shares could be set aside for purchase through volunteerism or "sweat equity," as it is sometimes called. Some synagogues own additional property, such as apartments in Israel, summer camps, and retreat centers, and might consider applying the time-share model to one of those properties.

A New Era for the Synagogue

This may be the end of the book, but it is only the beginning of a new era for the synagogue and the Jewish community. The synagogue has evolved since it was introduced to the Jewish community in the years prior to the destruction of the Second Temple in 70 CE. Following the destruction of the Temple, the synagogue became the primary Jewish communal institution dedicated to prayer and worship. As the centralized Jewish community began to unravel, smaller fragmented communities began to emerge, with the synagogue as their focal point. The synagogue as we know it differs greatly from the original synagogue, as does its rabbinic leadership. Both have changed as the needs of the Jewish community have changed, and there is no reason to believe the synagogue and the rabbinate will not continue to evolve. The only thing that we can be sure of is that the models for the synagogue that ultimately emerge will reflect the needs and wants of the majority of the community.

We are at a point in our history when change is once again required. At times this change will emerge on its own. At other times change will require making a deliberate response to the various cultural forces around us. However, we cannot wait for the surrounding culture to motivate the inevitable changes; rather, we have to shape the future as it unfolds in front of us. Whatever we call the financial relationship between synagogue users and the synagogue, these funds are an investment in the Jewish present and our guarantee for a secure and vital Jewish future.

If we are to truly embrace this era of synagogue transition, we have to be willing to take some risks. Those risks include what may be described as "betting the farm." In other words, if we make only small changes, the returns will also be small, if they appear at all. Instead, we have to make radical changes in the structure and organization of the synagogue, along with changes to membership and revenue models.

Synagogues—and other Jewish and secular communal institutions like them—have difficulty changing. Leaders will argue that synagogues have been around for decades and there is no reason to believe that they will not continue to exist. But synagogues today cannot survive on the institutional successes of the past. Nevertheless, they are indispensable to living a Jewish spiritual life. Rabbi Ammiel Hirsch of the Stephen Wise Free Synagogue in New York City aptly put it, "Synagogues are the anchoring institution of American Jewry."[5]

As folk wisdom teaches us, "If we don't know where we are going, any road will take us there." But we want to ensure that the forces that help us make decisions regarding synagogue change are not solely economic. Instead, they should come from deep-seated philosophical commitments to Jewish faith and community and a desire to open our doors into the Jewish community wider. Our future and the future of the synagogue are dependent on our ability to build a Jewish community where all are welcome, where no matter our background or subgroup we feel welcomed and embraced, where we feel that we belong—because we do.

May it be Your will, O our God,
that we may be allowed to stand in places of astonishing light
and not in dark places,

and may our hearts know no pain,

and may our vision not be so clouded
that we would not see all the blessings of Life
that You have given us.

Danny Siegel[1]
Adapted from Rabbi Alexandrai's or Rav Himnuna's prayer
Babylonian Talmud, *Berakhot* 17a

Afterword

The dues system that many synagogues presently use was not handed down at Mount Sinai. Neither was it included in the Talmud, nor prescribed in any of the major codes of Jewish law. There is nothing particularly ordained about this way of raising money for synagogues. While the dues system has been an important part of the success of synagogues in the twentieth century, the challenges facing many congregations in this twenty-first century may demand new solutions, and synagogues should not feel bound to what may not serve them. The great pleasure of reading this book is seeing the possibility and creativity of the institutions that the Olitzkys have identified.

The challenge for many synagogues, as the Olitzkys have adroitly shown, is figuring out whether they need to change. And if they need to change, what model should they employ? And should they do it in piecemeal fashion or change it all at once? But there is a question that even precedes these questions and is the reason I think many synagogues have recently changed financial and membership models. It is the question of what will happen if we don't change our membership and revenue model. What will our institution look like in five or ten years? Given demographic and economic trends, can we still be a vibrant institution that will provide a spiritual home for the next generation even if we don't change?

The problem for synagogues is that historically they are conservative and pragmatic when it comes to money and membership. If a synagogue has 500 families or even 1,000 families with an active board of directors and lots of different ideas about the Jewish future, it's not easy to get everyone together and tell the assembled group that the leadership of the synagogue is thinking about eliminating dues so that people can pay what they will. Similarly, it may not be easy to suggest that synagogue leaders want to merge buildings or Hebrew schools with a neighboring synagogue to gain economic efficiencies. But one of the values of this book is in seeing so many examples and the empirical evidence of congregations that have made precisely these changes and been strengthened as a result.

The original introduction of the dues system is an interesting case study in risk management. As the Olitzkys note early in this book, American congregations did not always rely on dues. The primary way synagogues financed themselves until around World War I was by selling seats. One would buy a seat and pay a yearly assessment on it in the same way one might buy a season ticket for professional football, and no one was allowed to sit in someone else's seat even if the ticket holder wasn't present at the game. Synagogues stopped using this system when the system stopped working. At the beginning of the twentieth century, Jews became less interested in buying permanent seats. Being able to pay for better seats was seen as elitist. Synagogue attendees saw the process as undemocratic, since some people were obviously able to afford more expensive seats than others. It became a barrier to joining a synagogue, something that synagogues assiduously wanted to avoid. The membership-and-dues model became a solution to this challenge. One price for membership that everyone pays. No more elitism. It was a risk for congregations to retire the previous system that had sustained them, but they knew that maintaining the status quo was even riskier. And the new system clearly worked for synagogues for a long time. But the notion of elitism and barriers to entry that haunted synagogues one hundred years ago has resurfaced. The membership-and-dues model that is commonplace in synagogues is seen once again as an elitist barrier to membership. New funding models have to change this so that congregations can be as embracing of members as possible.

When I was a congregational rabbi, I was always the so-called soft touch who was willing "to give away the house" when members approached me about financial problems that prevented them from paying what was perceived by our leadership as their share of dues. I had the most *mentshlikh* (kind) congregation in America, so they would say that they were happy their rabbi would be moved by people's problems, but I also had to understand, said these leaders, that the synagogue was a business and needed to make money to survive like any other business.

And they were not wrong. The synagogue did need funds to pay the bills. I would, however, suggest to these same leaders that if we were a business, like any good business, we needed to spend money to upgrade our websites, our facility, and our communications. This is what would make our institution attractive to potential members. At that point, the same board member who had just told me we were a business said, "Oh, Rabbi, that would cost a lot of money. We're not some business that can afford to spend like that." So a congregation is not a business, but exactly what should a synagogue be?

One of the problems with the membership-and-dues model in place in most synagogues is that it is, in many ways, akin to a business model. A member pays a fee and receives services in return. For many of our Protestant neighbors, for whom membership in a church is primarily a matter of belief, the financial commitment is an outgrowth of that belief. For Jews, membership is usually defined as having paid a membership fee. Yes, every congregation in America has something in their bylaws that says they will not turn anyone away for lack of finances. And I believe congregations live by this value standard. Nonetheless, the dues model fundamentally equates membership with money. This may not always be a negative; paying for something means that that something is taken seriously. But for many people, the membership-and-dues model suggests a vision for community that is based on a transactional model.

If we move away from the business and transactional model, however, and say that synagogues should function as an open nonprofit, it raises other serious questions. What do we do about people who use services that they don't pay for? (The classic free-rider problem, as an economist might put it.) Is there still a value in membership if it is not tied to services that one receives?

My own research into this last question suggests that if people care about their synagogue and are engaged in it, they will freely give to it, even if there are no longer obligatory dues. If we think about successful, open nonprofits as models for the synagogue, we find that they are generally vision-driven institutions that have a significant level of financial transparency and do an excellent job of nurturing donor relations. Congregations will have to follow suit and also exhibit financial transparency. As members are considered donors, congregations will have to build trust with them and become—to use a Christian term—"good stewards."

Congregations have work to do in order to continue to be financially viable. But membership, however it is conceived, is really not about money. Money is just a tool for synagogues to be able to do their sacred work in the world. The Olitzkys have written a book that understands this notion. They may not have solved all of the contemporary synagogue's financial problems, but they have certainly opened us all up to potential paths for congregations, many of which have been previously unseen. They have helped synagogues who will want to more closely align their vision with their approach to revenue and membership. The dues system may not have been handed down at Sinai or given over to us through the Talmud, but the need for Jews to be in community is certainly an ancient context bequeathed to us from our sacred tradition, and this book will help Jews continue that age-old need of sustaining just and embracing communities.

Rabbi Dan Judson
Faculty member, Hebrew College Rabbinical School
National consultant to the Reform movement
on issues of syngogue finance
Coauthor, *Are Voluntary Dues Right for Your Synagogue?*
(UJA-Federation of New York)

Determining the Appropriate Model for Your Synagogue—A Checklist

Prepared by Debbie Joseph[1]

Synagogues choose financial models based on desired goals. If the statements below apply to your synagogue, you may want to consider the models suggested following each statement.

We are looking for a financial model that will allow us to:

☐ **Create a community of "members" without setting a mandatory dues schedule**

Consider

Co-op Model	Open Membership
No Dues	Voluntary Dues

☐ **Create different categories of membership that include different sets of benefits**

Consider

Open Membership	Tiered Model
Special-Interest Membership	Transactional Membership

☐ **Create a menu of varying services and programs and charge fees only for these services**

Consider

Open Membership	Tiered Model
Special-Interest Membership	Transactional Membership

☐ **Open our synagogue doors for all to enter regardless of their ability to give**

Consider

Co-op Model	Open Membership
No Dues	Voluntary Dues

Synagogues choose financial models that are built upon their unique features. If the statements below describe your synagogue, you may want to consider the models suggested following each statement.

☐ **We have a reliable core of substantial donors.**

Consider

No Dues
No-Membership Model
Open Membership
Voluntary Dues

☐ **We have hallmark programs and services that draw beyond our membership.**

Consider

No Dues
No-Membership Model
Open Membership
Special-Interest Membership
Tiered Model
Voluntary Dues

☐ **We are fairly homogeneous in our demographics or heavily weighted in one or two age groups, interest groups, and/or geographic service areas.**

Consider

Open Membership
Special-Interest Membership
Tiered Model

☐ **We are very successful at fundraising and development.**

Consider

No Dues
No-Membership Model
Open Membership

☐ **We live in an area with several other Jewish organizations and we have a history of collaboration.**

Consider

Community Campus
Open Membership
Special-Interest Membership

Synagogues also choose revenue models that align with their vision and culture. If these statements reflect your vision and culture, you may want to consider the models suggested following each statement.

☐ **We strive to be a "relational" synagogue and place a value on connections with each other and with our community.**

Consider

Co-op Model
No Dues
No-Membership Model
Open Membership
Voluntary Dues

☐ **We are always looking for strategies to engage more people inside our synagogue as well as outside of our membership.**

Consider

Community Campus
No Dues
No-Membership Model
Open Membership
Special-Interest Membership
Tiered Model
Voluntary Dues

☐ **We believe that contributions of time and money are equally important.**

Consider

Co-op Model
No Dues
No-Membership Model
Open Membership
Voluntary Dues

☐ **We are looking to provide meaningful Jewish experiences for all people, including those who are not necessarily looking to "belong" to a synagogue.**

Consider

Community Campus
Co-op Model
No-Membership Model
Open Membership
Special-Interest Membership
Transactional Membership

Ten Things to Do Following the Decision to Adopt a New Membership or Revenue Model—A Checklist

Prepared by Debbie Joseph

☐ 1. Add a page to the synagogue website that clearly explains your new membership model, including what it is called, why you chose it, and how it works.

☐ 2. Create a list of Frequently Asked Questions (FAQs) and make it available in multiple locations, including your website, newsletter, synagogue office, and new member packets.

☐ 3. Update all marketing and communication materials that include membership information, and create at least one new flyer, ad, brochure, or pamphlet featuring your new membership model.

☐ 4. Conduct a town hall meeting or congregational forum to give members an opportunity to ask questions and share feedback about the new model.

☐ 5. Reach out individually to key stakeholders, affiliate presidents, and others to garner support for the new model.

☐ 6. Report on the impact of the new model at every board meeting.

☐ 7. Create easy-to-use pledge forms, membership applications, payment schedules, and payment options.

☐ 8. Train all staff members and volunteer leaders on how to describe the new model to current and potential new members.

☐ 9. Draft a press release for local media.

☐ 10. Develop an evaluation plan to measure the success of your new model.

Twenty-Five Reasons to Join Synagogues

A synagogue is the place where ...

1. We can encounter God, engage with God, wrestle with God.
2. We can hear God's voice without the intrusion of the world's noise around us.
3. We can say prayers for healing and find personal healing of the soul.
4. We can pray with a community that supports and nurtures us.
5. We can find answers to the big questions in life.
6. We can find help formulating the questions.
7. We can find an anchor in a rudderless world.
8. We can be lifted up when we fall.
9. We can be taught to be humble.
10. We can learn to express gratitude.
11. We can intimately connect to Jewish religion or religious practice where it is preserved along with its contemporary expression.
12. We can mark the transitions of life.
13. We can educate our children and grandchildren.
14. We can learn Hebrew and learn about Judaism and Jewish religious practice.

15. We can learn the Torah of living a righteous and fulfilling life.
16. We can discover our place in the collective history of the Jewish people, as well as determine our role in it.
17. We can find affinity with others who hold values similar to our own.
18. We can hear a message of hope we can offer to the greater community.
19. Our children can be taught to be *menschen*, moral and upstanding contributors to society, and taught a values system to make their own moral and ethical decisions.
20. We can find a community of transcendent meaning and at the same time be intellectually stimulated Jewishly.
21. We can explore and deepen our relationship with the land and people of Israel.
22. We can make a statement to our neighbors about the rightful, equal place of Jews in society, as well as the importance of Judaism and Jewishness for our own identity and the identity of our families.
23. We can organize and be organized around societal and social justice issues that affect us and our community, and we can volunteer to help others in need.
24. We can participate in Jewish cultural and social, as well as religious, activities.
25. We can develop and offer our leadership to the Jewish community and the Jewish people.

Notes

Foreword

1. Rabbi Lawrence S. Kushner has served as the Emanu-El Scholar at Congregation Emanu-El in San Francisco, California, since 2002. Rabbi Kushner served for twenty-eight years as the rabbi of Congregation Beth El in Sudbury, Massachusetts, and is the author of many groundbreaking books on Jewish mysticism. For more of Lawrence Kushner's thoughts on congregations, see *I'm God; You're Not: Observations on Organized Religion & Other Disguises of the Ego* (Woodstock, VT: Jewish Lights, 2010).
2. Heard in a sermon by Rabbi Feinstein.

Introduction

1. Lawrence Kushner, *I'm God; You're Not: Observations on Organized Religion & Other Disguises of the Ego* (Woodstock, VT: Jewish Lights, 2010), 22.
2. Pew Research Center, "A Portrait of American Jews: Findings from a Pew Research Center Survey of U.S. Jews," October 1, 2013. The full report is available online at www.pewforum.org/files/2013/10/jewish-american-full-report-for-web.pdf.
3. United Jewish Communities, "National Jewish Population Survey 2000–01: Strength, Challenge, and Diversity in the American Jewish Population," September 2003, updated January 2004. The full report is available online at www.jewishdatabank.org/Studies/downloadFile.cfm?FileID=1490.
4. Most notably, the two studies differed in the way a Jewish person was defined (Pew had a broader, more inclusive definition), and in the way the researchers went about gathering the information about respondents' Jewish identity (NJPS asked the question in an open-ended fashion, whereas Pew asked respondents to select from a list of religious identities).

1. The Shifting Relationship of the Synagogue and the Jewish Community

1. Amichai Lau-Lavie, "Why Synagogue? Thinking Out Loud About the Shifting Realities of Sacred Space," Lab/Shul blog, February 7, 2014, http://labshul.org/why-synagogue-thinking-out-loud-about-the-shifting-realities-of-sacred-space/2266. Amichai Lau-Lavie is the founder of Storahtelling (an educational drama troupe that interprets the weekly Torah reading) and the Lab/Shul in Manhattan. He is now a rabbinical student at The Jewish Theological Seminary.
2. Ron Wolfson, "Creating a Healthy Congregation: Interview with Ron Wolfson," *Reform Judaism*, Summer 2014, 39–40, 48.
3. Eric Yoffie, "Contemplations: An Interview with Rabbi Eric H. Yoffie," *Reform Judaism*, Spring 2012, 28–34.
4. "Membership," Congregation Beth Adam, http://bethadam.org/about/membership/.
5. Jeff Goldwasser, "Temple Dues and Don'ts," *Reb Jeff*, July 30, 2013, www.rebjeff.com/blog/temple-dues-and-donts.

2. Voluntary Dues

1. Peter S. Knobel, "Sacred Space Is Where God Dwells and Hearts Are Moved," ReformJudaism.org, www.reformjudaism.org/learning/torah-study/trumah/sacred-space-where-god-dwells-and-hearts-are-moved. Rabbi Peter S. Knobel is rabbi emeritus of Beth Emet: The Free Synagogue in Evanston, Illinois, and past president of the Central Conference of American Rabbis.
2. "Ohavi Zedek Synagogue Membership Financial Support Guidelines 5774 (2013–2014)," Ohavi Zedek Synagogue website, http://ohavizedek.org/wp-content/uploads/2014/10/Ohavi-Zedek-Membership-Support-Guidelines-5774-2013-4.pdf.
3. "TBA Potential/New Member FAQ," Temple Brith Achim website, www.brithachim.org/faq.html.
4. "*T'rumah,*" Temple Tifereth Israel Synagogue website, www.tiferethisrael.com/trumah/.
5. "Frequently Asked Questions about Membership," Temple B'nai Or website, http://templebnaior.org/join/faq/.
6. Ibid.
7. Temple Emanu-El website, http://emanu-el.org/.

8. "Congregation Beth Am New Dues Structure 2014–2015," Congregation Beth Am website, www.congregation-betham.org/_data/docs/14-15%20cba%20affordable%20membership%20initiative.pdf.
9. "Member Sign Up," Congregation Bet Shalom website, https://cbsaz.clubexpress.com/content.aspx?page_id=60&club_id=161388&sl=342599213.

3. No Dues or "Gifts of the Heart"

1. Isaac Mayer Wise, *American Israelite*, July 29, 1887. Rabbi Isaac Mayer Wise founded the three major institutions of the Reform movement in North America: the Central Conference for American Rabbis, Hebrew Union College (now Hebrew Union College–Jewish Institute of Religion), and the Union of American Hebrew Congregations (now the Union for Reform Judaism).
2. Lawrence A. Hoffman, *Rethinking Synagogues: A New Vocabulary for Congregational Life* (Woodstock, VT: Jewish Lights, 2006), 90. Rabbi Lawrence A. Hoffman is the Barbara and Stephen Friedman Professor of Liturgy, Worship, and Ritual at Hebrew Union College–Jewish Institute of Religion, New York, and the author of over forty books.
3. "Membership," The New Shul website, http://thenewshul.org/membership/.
4. Correspondence with Rabbi Michael Wasserman, November 5, 2014.
5. "Get Involved," Mitziut website, http://mitziut.weebly.com/get-involved.html.
6. "Support Our Work," Mitziut website, http://mitziut.weebly.com/support-our-work.html.
7. Ibid.

4. Transactional Membership

1. Rabbi Elliot J. Cosgrove, "Why Synagogue?" February 1, 2014, http://pasyn.org/resources/sermons/why-synagogue. Rabbi Elliot Cosgrove is the rabbi of Park Avenue Synagogue in New York City.
2. "Join/Enroll," Tamid: The Downtown Synagogue website, http://tamidnyc.org/joinenroll/.

5. Open Membership

1. Rabbi Mordecai Yosef Leiner of Izbica was a nineteenth-century Polish rabbi who founded the Izbica-Radzyn dynasty of Hasidic Judaism.
2. David Cohen, "Why Belong to a Synagogue?" *Wisconsin Jewish Chronicle,* June 2010, www.congregationsinai.com/rabbi-cohens-sermons/134-why-synagogue. Rabbi David Cohen is rabbi of Congregation Sinai in Milwaukee, Wisconsin.
3. Andrew Fluegelman, quoted in "PC-Talk," by Lawrence J. Magid, *PC Magazine*, August 1982, 143.

6. The No-Membership Model

1. As quoted by Alan Temperow in "Join a Synagogue for the 'Fringe' Benefits" www.shalomboston.com/linkclick.aspx?fileticket=4ntzgp89Huk= (Accessed December 17, 2014). Rabbi Alexander Schindler (1925–2000) was the president of the Union for Reform Judaism (formerly the Union of American Hebrew Congregations) from 1973 to 1996.
2. David A. Teutsch, *Spiritual Community: The Power to Restore Hope, Commitment and Joy* (Woodstock, VT: Jewish Lights, 2005), 81. Rabbi David A. Teutsch was president of the Reconstructionist Rabbinical College and continues to serve on its faculty as the Louis and Myra Wiener Professor of Contemporary Jewish Civilization. He serves as the director of its Levin-Lieber Program in Jewish Ethics. He is the author of numerous books and editor in chief of the *Kol Haneshamah* prayer book series.
3. "About Us," Manhattan Jewish Experience website, https://jewishexperience.org/about-us.
4. Tom Tugend, "If You Stream Kol Nidre, They Will Watch," *Jewish Journal*, October 23, 2008, www.jewishjournal.com/religion/article/if_you_stream_kol_nidre_they_will_watch_20081022.
5. "Team 6," Sixth & I website, https://action.sixthandi.org/team6/.

7. The Tiered Model

1. Alan Teperow, "Join a Synagogue for the Fringe Benefits," ShalomBoston, www.shalomboston.com/linkclick.aspx?fileticket=4ntzgp89Huk=.

Alan Teperow is executive director of the Synagogue Council of Massachusetts and managing director of the Massachusetts Board of Rabbis.

2. Adam J. Raskin, "Ten Truths of Synagogue Life," *CJ: Voices of Conservative/Masorti Judaism,* www.cjvoices.org/article/ten-truths-of-synagogue-life/. Rabbi Adam J. Raskin is senior rabbi of Congregation Har Shalom in Potomac, Maryland.
3. "Membership," Temple Beth Hillel–Beth El website, www.tbhbe.org/membership-2/.
4. "Museum Membership," American Alliance of Museums website, www.aam-us.org/membership/member-types-and-benefits/museum-membership.

8. Special-Interest Membership

1. Harold M. Schulweis, "The Synagogue as a Therapeutic Community," Valley Beth Shalom website, www.vbs.org/page.cfm?p=830. Rabbi Harold M. Schulweis (*z"l*) served as a rabbi at Valley Beth Shalom in Encino, California, from 1970 to 2014. He is the author of numerous books, including *Conscience: The Duty to Obey and the Duty to Disobey* (Woodstock, VT: Jewish Lights, 2008).
2. Ronen Neuwirth, "The 'Ten Commandments' for Making Synagogues More Welcoming Places for Secular Jews," *Jerusalem Post*, September 27, 2014, www.jpost.com/Opinion/The-Ten-Commandments-for-making-synagogues-more-welcoming-places-for-secular-Jews-376436. Rabbi Ronen Neuwirth is the rabbi of Ohel Ari Congregation in Ra'anana, Israel, and the director of Beit Hillel, a Modern Orthodox spiritual leadership organization.
3. "About Lab/Shul," Lab/Shul website, http://labshul.org/about-labshul/.
4. "Membership Services," IEEE South Saskatchewan website, http://sosask.ieee.ca/membership.html.

9. The Community Campus

1. Kirk Wisemayer, "Coming Together as 'One Jewish Community,'" *Jewish Community Voice* 74, no. 6 (October 29, 2014), www.jewishvoicesnj.org/news/2014-07-09/Voice_at_the_Shore/Coming_Together_as_One_Jewish_Community.html. Kirk Wisemayer is acting executive director of the Jewish Federation of Atlantic & Cape May Counties, New Jersey.

2. "Welcome to Makom Hadash," Makom Hadash website, http://makomhadash.org/.
3. Ibid.

10. The Co-op Model

1. Rabbi Jack Reimer is a well-known author and speaker. He founded the National Rabbinic Network, a support system for rabbis across denominational lines, and is the coeditor of *Ethical Wills and How to Prepare Them: A Guide to Sharing Your Values from Generation to Generation* (Woodstock, VT: Jewish Lights, 2015).
2. Kavana Cooperative website, www.kavana.org/.
3. "Kavana Partnership Explained," Kavana Cooperative website, www.kavana.org/kavana-partnership-explained.
4. "Our Vision," Jewish Collaborative of San Diego website, www.jcosd.com/the-jewish-collaborative-of-san-diego/.
5. "Our Mission," Jewish Collaborative of San Diego website, www.jcosd.com/an-alternatively-organized-jewish-community/.

11. The Hybrid Model

1. Randall J. Konigsburg, "Growing a Synagogue Part Six—Some Final Thoughts," *Jewish Common Sense* (blog), November 7, 2011, http://commonsensejews.blogspot.com/2011/11/growing-synagogue-part-six-some-final.html. Rabbi Randall J. Konigsburg is senior rabbi at Temple Beth-El in Birmingham, Alabama.
2. "Who We Are," Congregation Dorshei Tzedek website, http://dorsheitzedek.org/who-we-are.
3. "Welcome to The Community Synagogue," The Community Synagogue website, http://commsyn.org/welcome-3.

Conclusion

1. Carol Ochs, *Our Lives as Torah: Finding God in Our Own Stories* (San Francisco: Jossey-Bass, 2001), 154. Dr. Carol Ochs is former director of the graduate studies program at Hebrew Union College–Jewish Institute of Religion, which she served as a spiritual director. She is the author of numerous books.
2. Steven Moskowitz, "Spotify and Synagogues: A Meditation on the Synagogue," September 27, 2014, www.rabbimoskowitz.com/2014/09/spotify-and-synagogues-meditation-on.html. Rabbi Steven Moskowitz

is rabbi of the Jewish Congregation of Brookville and the Oyster Bay Jewish Center, a joined community serving the North Shore of Long Island, New York.

3. Kehilat Hadar website, www.kehilathadar.org/.
4. "Our Rabbi," Mishkan Chicago website, www.mishkanchicago.org/who-we-are/our-rabbi/.
5. Ammiel Hirsch, "The Pew Survey of U.S. Jews: Ramifications and Recommendations," *The Blog, Huffington Post*, October 7, 2013, www.huffingtonpost.com/rabbi-ammiel-hirsch/pew-survey-jewish-americans_b_4057905.html.

Afterword

1. Danny Siegel, "May it be Your will, O our God, that we may be allowed to stand in places of astonishing light," *Healing: Readings and Meditations* (Pittsboro, NC: Town House Press, 1999). Danny Siegel is a well-known author, lecturer, and poet. He is the author of thirty books and founder of the Ziv Tzedakah Fund.

Determining the Appropriate Model for Your Synagogue

1. Debbie Joseph is founder and president of Debbie Joseph Consulting, Inc. She specializes in helping synagogues explore and adopt alternative membership and revenue models.

Resources

Books

Aron, Isa. *Becoming a Congregation of Learners: Learning as a Key to Revitalizing Congregational Life*. Woodstock, VT: Jewish Lights, 2000.

________. *The Self-Renewing Congregation: Organizational Strategies for Revitalizing Congregational Life*. Woodstock, VT: Jewish Lights, 2002.

Aron, Isa, Steven M. Cohen, Lawrence A. Hoffman, and Ari Y. Kelman. *Sacred Strategies: Transforming Synagogues from Functional to Visionary*. Bethesda, MD: Alban Institute, 2010.

Bookman, Terry, and William Kahn. *This House We Build: Lessons for Healthy Synagogues and the People Who Dwell There*. Bethesda, MD: Alban Institute, 2007.

Chernov, Beryl P., Debbie Joseph, and Daniel Judson. *Are Voluntary Dues Right for Your Synagogue? A Practical Guide.* Innovation and Strategies for Synagogues of Tomorrow, vol. 8. New York: UJA–Federation of New York, 2015.

HaLevi, Baruch, and Ellen Frankel. *Revolution of Jewish Spirit: How to Revive Ruakh in Your Spiritual Life, Transform Your Synagogue & Inspire Your Jewish Community*. Woodstock, VT: Jewish Lights, 2012.

Heller, Zachary I., ed. *Synagogues in a Time of Change: Fragmentation and Diversity in Jewish Religious Movements*. Bethesda, MD: Alban Institute, 2009.

Herring, Hayim. *Tomorrow's Synagogue Today: Creating Vibrant Centers of Jewish Life*. Bethesda, MD: Alban Institute, 2012.

Hoffman, Lawrence A. *Rethinking Synagogues: A New Vocabulary for Congregational Life*. Woodstock, VT: Jewish Lights, 2006.

Kaunfer, Elie. *Empowered Judaism: What Independent Minyanim Can Teach Us about Building Vibrant Jewish Communities*. Woodstock, VT: Jewish Lights, 2010.

Leventhal, Robert. *Stepping Forward: Synagogue Visioning and Planning*. Bethesda, MD: Alban Institute, 2007.

Olitzky, Kerry. *Playlist Judaism: Making Choices for a Vital Future*. Bethesda, MD: Alban Institute, 2013.

Schwarz, Sid. *Finding a Spiritual Home: How a New Generation of Jews Can Transform the American Synagogue*. Woodstock, VT: Jewish Lights, 2003.

———. *Jewish Megatrends: Charting the Course of the American Jewish Future.* Woodstock, VT: Jewish Lights, 2013.

Teutsch, David A. *Spiritual Community: The Power to Restore Hope, Commitment and Joy*. Woodstock, VT: Jewish Lights, 2005.

Wolfson, Ron. *Relational Judaism: Using the Power of Relationships to Transform the Jewish Community*. Woodstock, VT: Jewish Lights, 2013.

———. *The Spirituality of Welcoming: How to Transform Your Congregation into a Sacred Community*. Woodstock, VT: Jewish Lights, 2006.

Zevit, Shawn Israel. *Offerings of the Heart: Money and Values in Faith Communities*. Bethesda, MD: Alban Institute, 2005.

Organizations

Center for Congregations
303 North Alabama Street, Suite 100
Indianapolis, IN 46204
(866) 307-2381
www.centerforcongregations.org

Synagogue Leadership Initiative
Jewish Federation of Northern New Jersey
50 Eisenhower Drive
Paramus, NJ 07652
(201) 820-3901
www.jfnnj.org/sli

Synergy: UJA-Federation of New York and Synagogues Together
130 East 59th Street
New York, NY 10022
(212) 836-1832
www.ujafedny.org/synergy/

Inspiration

The Chutzpah Imperative: Empowering Today's Jews for a Life That Matters *By Rabbi Edward Feinstein; Foreword by Rabbi Laura Geller*
A new view of chutzpah as Jewish self-empowerment to be God's partner and repair the world. Reveals Judaism's ancient message, its deepest purpose and most precious treasures. 6 x 9, 192 pp, HC, 978-1-58023-792-5 **$21.99**

Judaism's Ten Best Ideas: A Brief Guide for Seekers
By Rabbi Arthur Green, PhD A highly accessible introduction to Judaism's greatest contributions to civilization, drawing on Jewish mystical tradition and the author's experience. 4½ x 6½, 112 pp, Quality PB, 978-1-58023-803-8 **$9.99**

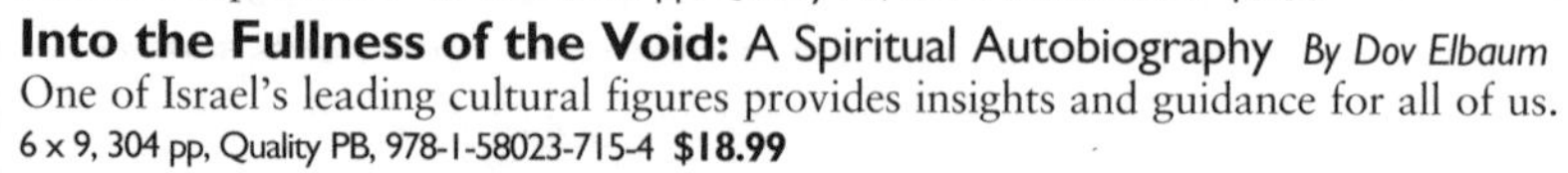

Into the Fullness of the Void: A Spiritual Autobiography *By Dov Elbaum*
One of Israel's leading cultural figures provides insights and guidance for all of us.
6 x 9, 304 pp, Quality PB, 978-1-58023-715-4 **$18.99**

The Bridge to Forgiveness: Stories and Prayers for Finding God and Restoring Wholeness
By Rabbi Karyn D. Kedar 6 x 9, 176 pp, Quality PB, 978-1-58023-451-1 **$16.99**

The Empty Chair: Finding Hope and Joy—Timeless Wisdom from a Hasidic Master, Rebbe Nachman of Breslov *Adapted by Moshe Mykoff and the Breslov Research Institute*
4 x 6, 128 pp, Deluxe PB w/ flaps, 978-1-879045-67-5 **$9.99**

The Gentle Weapon: Prayers for Everyday and Not-So-Everyday Moments—Timeless Wisdom from the Teachings of the Hasidic Master Rebbe Nachman of Breslov
Adapted by Moshe Mykoff and S. C. Mizrahi, together with the Breslov Research Institute
4 x 6, 144 pp, Deluxe PB w/ flaps, 978-1-58023-022-3 **$9.99**

God Whispers: Stories of the Soul, Lessons of the Heart *By Rabbi Karyn D. Kedar*
6 x 9, 176 pp, Quality PB, 978-1-58023-088-9 **$16.99**

God's To-Do List: 103 Ways to Be an Angel and Do God's Work on Earth
By Dr. Ron Wolfson 6 x 9, 144 pp, Quality PB, 978-1-58023-301-9 **$16.99**

Happiness and the Human Spirit: The Spirituality of Becoming the Best You Can Be
By Rabbi Abraham J. Twerski, MD
6 x 9, 176 pp, Quality PB, 978-1-58023-404-7 **$16.99**; HC, 978-1-58023-343-9 **$19.99**

Life's Daily Blessings: Inspiring Reflections on Gratitude and Joy for Every Day, Based on Jewish Wisdom *By Rabbi Kerry M. Olitzky* 4½ x 6½, 368 pp, Quality PB, 978-1-58023-396-5 **$16.99**

Restful Reflections: Nighttime Inspiration to Calm the Soul, Based on Jewish Wisdom
By Rabbi Kerry M. Olitzky and Rabbi Lori Forman-Jacobi
4½ x 6½, 448 pp, Quality PB, 978-1-58023-091-9 **$16.99**

Sacred Intentions: Morning Inspiration to Strengthen the Spirit, Based on Jewish Wisdom
By Rabbi Kerry M. Olitzky and Rabbi Lori Forman-Jacobi
4½ x 6½, 448 pp, Quality PB, 978-1-58023-061-2 **$16.99**

Saying No and Letting Go: Jewish Wisdom on Making Room for What Matters Most
By Rabbi Edwin Goldberg, DHL; Foreword by Rabbi Naomi Levy
6 x 9, 192 pp, Quality PB, 978-1-58023-670-6 **$16.99**

The Seven Questions You're Asked in Heaven: Reviewing and Renewing Your Life on Earth *By Dr. Ron Wolfson* 6 x 9, 176 pp, Quality PB, 978-1-58023-407-8 **$16.99**

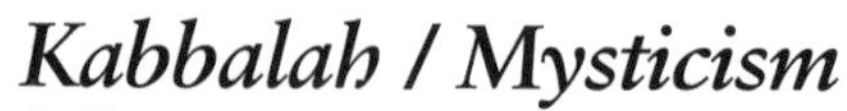

Kabbalah / Mysticism

Ehyeh: A Kabbalah for Tomorrow
By Rabbi Arthur Green, PhD 6 x 9, 224 pp, Quality PB, 978-1-58023-213-5 **$18.99**

The Gift of Kabbalah: Discovering the Secrets of Heaven, Renewing Your Life on Earth
By Tamar Frankiel, PhD 6 x 9, 256 pp, Quality PB, 978-1-58023-141-1 **$18.99**

Jewish Mysticism and the Spiritual Life: Classical Texts, Contemporary Reflections *Edited by Dr. Lawrence Fine, Dr. Eitan Fishbane and Rabbi Or N. Rose*
6 x 9, 256 pp, HC, 978-1-58023-434-4 **$24.99**; Quality PB, 978-1-58023-719-2 **$18.99**

Seek My Face: A Jewish Mystical Theology *By Rabbi Arthur Green, PhD*
6 x 9, 304 pp, Quality PB, 978-1-58023-130-5 **$19.95**

Zohar: Annotated & Explained *Translation & Annotation by Dr. Daniel C. Matt*
Foreword by Andrew Harvey 5½ x 8½, 176 pp, Quality PB, 978-1-893361-51-5 **$18.99**
(A book from SkyLight Paths, Jewish Lights' sister imprint)

Spirituality

Amazing *Chesed*: Living a Grace-Filled Judaism
By Rabbi Rami Shapiro Drawing from ancient and contemporary, traditional and non-traditional Jewish wisdom, reclaims the idea of grace in Judaism.
6 x 9, 176 pp, Quality PB, 978-1-58023-624-9 **$16.99**

Jewish with Feeling: A Guide to Meaningful Jewish Practice
By Rabbi Zalman Schachter-Shalomi (z"l) with Joel Segel
Takes off from basic questions like "Why be Jewish?" and whether the word *God* still speaks to us today and lays out a vision for a whole-person Judaism.
5½ x 8½, 288 pp, Quality PB, 978-1-58023-691-1 **$19.99**

Perennial Wisdom for the Spiritually Independent: Sacred Teachings—Annotated & Explained *Annotation by Rabbi Rami Shapiro; Foreword by Richard Rohr*
Weaves sacred texts and teachings from the world's major religions into a coherent exploration of the five core questions at the heart of every religion's search.
5½ x 8½, 336 pp, Quality PB, 978-1-59473-515-8 **$16.99**

A Book of Life: Embracing Judaism as a Spiritual Practice
By Rabbi Michael Strassfeld 6 x 9, 544 pp, Quality PB, 978-1-58023-247-0 **$24.99**

Bringing the Psalms to Life: How to Understand and Use the Book of Psalms
By Rabbi Daniel F. Polish, PhD 6 x 9, 208 pp, Quality PB, 978-1-58023-157-2 **$18.99**

Does the Soul Survive? 2nd Edition: A Jewish Journey to Belief in Afterlife, Past Lives & Living with Purpose *By Rabbi Elie Kaplan Spitz; Foreword by Brian L. Weiss, MD*
6 x 9, 288 pp, Quality PB, 978-1-58023-818-2 **$18.99**

Entering the Temple of Dreams: Jewish Prayers, Movements and Meditations for the End of the Day *By Tamar Frankiel, PhD, and Judy Greenfeld*
7 x 10, 192 pp, illus., Quality PB, 978-1-58023-079-7 **$16.95**

First Steps to a New Jewish Spirit: Reb Zalman's Guide to Recapturing the Intimacy & Ecstasy in Your Relationship with God
By Rabbi Zalman Schachter-Shalomi (z"l) with Donald Gropman
6 x 9, 144 pp, Quality PB, 978-1-58023-182-4 **$16.95**

Foundations of Sephardic Spirituality: The Inner Life of Jews of the Ottoman Empire
By Rabbi Marc D. Angel, PhD 6 x 9, 224 pp, Quality PB, 978-1-58023-341-5 **$18.99**

God & the Big Bang: Discovering Harmony between Science & Spirituality
By Dr. Daniel C. Matt 6 x 9, 216 pp, Quality PB, 978-1-879045-89-7 **$18.99**

God in Our Relationships: Spirituality between People from the Teachings of Martin Buber
By Rabbi Dennis S. Ross 5½ x 8½, 160 pp, Quality PB, 978-1-58023-147-3 **$16.95**

The God Upgrade: Finding Your 21st-Century Spirituality in Judaism's 5,000-Year-Old Tradition *By Rabbi Jamie Korngold; Foreword by Rabbi Harold M. Schulweis*
6 x 9, 176 pp, Quality PB, 978-1-58023-443-6 **$15.99**

The Jewish Lights Spirituality Handbook: A Guide to Understanding, Exploring & Living a Spiritual Life *Edited by Stuart M. Matlins*
6 x 9, 456 pp, Quality PB, 978-1-58023-093-3 **$19.99**

Judaism, Physics and God: Searching for Sacred Metaphors in a Post-Einstein World
By Rabbi David W. Nelson
6 x 9, 352 pp, Quality PB, inc. reader's discussion guide, 978-1-58023-306-4 **$18.99**
HC, 352 pp, 978-1-58023-252-4 **$24.99**

Repentance: The Meaning and Practice of Teshuvah
By Dr. Louis E. Newman; Foreword by Rabbi Harold M. Schulweis; Preface by Rabbi Karyn D. Kedar
6 x 9, 256 pp, HC, 978-1-58023-426-9 **$24.99**; Quality PB, 978-1-58023-718-5 **$18.99**

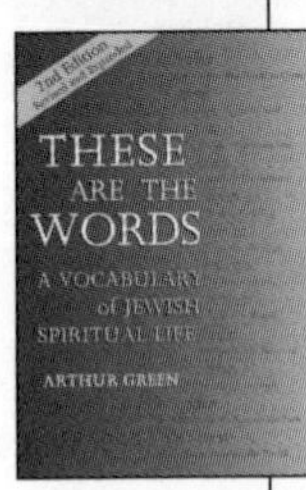

The Sabbath Soul: Mystical Reflections on the Transformative Power of Holy Time
Selection, Translation and Commentary by Eitan Fishbane, PhD
6 x 9, 208 pp, Quality PB, 978-1-58023-459-7 **$18.99**

***Tanya*, the Masterpiece of Hasidic Wisdom:** Selections Annotated & Explained
Translation & Annotation by Rabbi Rami Shapiro; Foreword by Rabbi Zalman Schachter-Shalomi (z"l)
5½ x 8½, 240 pp, Quality PB, 978-1-59473-275-1 **$18.99**

These Are the Words, 2nd Edition: A Vocabulary of Jewish Spiritual Life
By Rabbi Arthur Green, PhD 6 x 9, 320 pp, Quality PB, 978-1-58023-494-8 **$19.99**

Congregation Resources

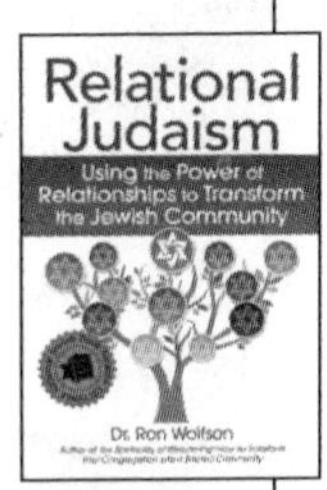

Relational Judaism: Using the Power of Relationships to Transform the Jewish Community *By Dr. Ron Wolfson* How to transform the model of twentieth-century Jewish institutions into twenty-first-century relational communities offering meaning and purpose, belonging and blessing.
6 x 9, 288 pp, HC, 978-1-58023-666-9 **$24.99**

The Spirituality of Welcoming: How to Transform Your Congregation into a Sacred Community *By Dr. Ron Wolfson*
Shows crucial hospitality is for congregational survival and dives into the practicalities of cultivating openness. 6 x 9, 224 pp, Quality PB, 978-1-58023-244-9 **$19.99**

Jewish Megatrends: Charting the Course of the American Jewish Future
By Rabbi Sidney Schwarz; Foreword by Ambassador Stuart E. Eizenstat
Visionary solutions for a community ripe for transformational change—from fourteen leading innovators of Jewish life. 6 x 9, 288 pp, HC, 978-1-58023-667-6 **$24.99**

Inspired Jewish Leadership: Practical Approaches to Building Strong Communities *By Dr. Erica Brown*
Develop your leadership skills and dialogue with others about issues like conflict resolution and effective succession planning.
6 x 9, 256 pp, HC, 978-1-58023-361-3 **$27.99**

Building a Successful Volunteer Culture: Finding Meaning in Service in the Jewish Community *By Rabbi Charles Simon; Foreword by Shelley Lindauer; Preface by Dr. Ron Wolfson*
6 x 9, 192 pp, Quality PB, 978-1-58023-408-5 **$16.99**

The Case for Jewish Peoplehood: Can We Be One?
By Dr. Erica Brown and Dr. Misha Galperin; Foreword by Rabbi Joseph Telushkin
6 x 9, 224 pp, HC, 978-1-58023-401-6 **$21.99**

Empowered Judaism: What Independent Minyanim Can Teach Us about Building Vibrant Jewish Communities *By Rabbi Elie Kaunfer; Foreword by Prof. Jonathan D. Sarna*
6 x 9, 224 pp, Quality PB, 978-1-58023-412-2 **$18.99**

Finding a Spiritual Home: How a New Generation of Jews Can Transform the American Synagogue *By Rabbi Sidney Schwarz*
6 x 9, 352 pp, Quality PB, 978-1-58023-185-5 **$19.95**

Judaism and Health: A Handbook of Practical, Professional and Scholarly Resources
Edited by Jeff Levin, PhD, MPH, and Michele F. Prince, LCSW, MAJCS
Foreword by Rabbi Elliot N. Dorff, PhD
6 x 9, 448 pp, HC, 978-1-58023-714-7 **$50.00**

Jewish Pastoral Care, 2nd Edition: A Practical Handbook from Traditional & Contemporary Sources *Edited by Rabbi Dayle A. Friedman, MSW, MA, BCC*
6 x 9, 528 pp, Quality PB, 978-1-58023-427-6 **$40.00**

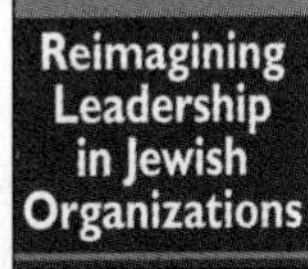

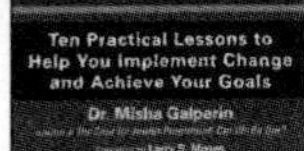

Jewish Spiritual Direction: An Innovative Guide from Traditional and Contemporary Sources *Edited by Rabbi Howard A. Addison, PhD, and Barbara Eve Breitman, MSW*
6 x 9, 368 pp, HC, 978-1-58023-230-2 **$30.00**

A Practical Guide to Rabbinic Counseling
Edited by Rabbi Yisrael N. Levitz, PhD, and Rabbi Abraham J. Twerski, MD
6 x 9, 432 pp, HC, 978-1-58023-562-4 **$40.00**

Professional Spiritual & Pastoral Care: A Practical Clergy and Chaplain's Handbook
Edited by Rabbi Stephen B. Roberts, MBA, MHL, BCJC
6 x 9, 480 pp, HC, 978-1-59473-312-3 **$50.00***

Reimagining Leadership in Jewish Organizations: Ten Practical Lessons to Help You Implement Change and Achieve Your Goals
By Dr. Misha Galperin 6 x 9, 192 pp, Quality PB, 978-1-58023-492-4 **$16.99**

Rethinking Synagogues: A New Vocabulary for Congregational Life
By Rabbi Lawrence A. Hoffman, PhD 6 x 9, 240 pp, Quality PB, 978-1-58023-248-7 **$19.99**

Revolution of Jewish Spirit: How to Revive *Ruakh* in Your Spiritual Life, Transform Your Synagogue & Inspire Your Jewish Community
By Rabbi Baruch HaLevi, DMin, and Ellen Frankel, LCSW; Foreword by Dr. Ron Wolfson
6 x 9, 224 pp, Quality PB, 978-1-58023-625-6 **$19.99**

**A book from SkyLight Paths, Jewish Lights' sister imprint*

About Jewish Lights

People of all faiths and backgrounds yearn for books that attract, engage, educate, and spiritually inspire.

Our principal goal is to stimulate thought and help all people learn about who the Jewish People are, where they come from, and what the future can be made to hold. While people of our diverse Jewish heritage are the primary audience, our books speak to people in the Christian world as well and will broaden their understanding of Judaism and the roots of their own faith.

We bring to you authors who are at the forefront of spiritual thought and experience. While each has something different to say, they all say it in a voice that you can hear.

Our books are designed to welcome you and then to engage, stimulate, and inspire. We judge our success not only by whether or not our books are beautiful and commercially successful, but by whether or not they make a difference in your life.

For your information and convenience, at the back of this book we have provided a list of other Jewish Lights books you might find interesting and useful. They cover all the categories of your life:

- Bar/Bat Mitzvah
- Bible Study / Midrash
- Children's Books
- Congregation Resources
- Current Events / History
- Ecology / Environment
- Fiction: Mystery, Science Fiction
- Grief / Healing
- Holidays / Holy Days
- Inspiration
- Kabbalah / Mysticism / Enneagram
- Life Cycle
- Meditation
- Men's Interest
- Parenting
- Prayer / Ritual / Sacred Practice
- Social Justice
- Spirituality
- Theology / Philosophy
- Travel
- Twelve Steps
- Women's Interest

Stuart M. Matlins, Publisher